RAISING
KIDS
WHO
HUNGER
FOR GOD

RAISING
KIDS
WHO
HUNGER
FOR GOD

Benny &
Sheree
Phillips

Chosen Books

A Division of Baker Book House Co
Grand Rapids, Michigan 49516

Library of Congress Cataloging-in-Publication Data

Phillips, Benny.
    Raising kids who hunger for God / Benny & Sheree Phillips.
      p. cm.
    ISBN 0-8007-9181-9
    1. Parenting—Religious aspects—Christianity. 2. Child rearing—Religious aspects—Christianity. 3. Children—Religious life. I. Phillips, Sheree. II. Title.
BV4526.2.P455   1991
248.8'45—dc20   91-7367
                                       CIP

Sixth printing, September 1996

Printed in the United States of America

To
Joshua, Jaime, Jesse, Joseph, Janelle and Jacob—
the six arrows we've been given to fashion for God.

Acknowledgments

We would like to thank the following people who served us unselfishly through the months of completing this project:

Mom, for your untiring willingness to spend time with the children. Your love and availability to us means more than we can express. We love you!

Josh and Jaime, for spending so many of your summer days caring cheerfully for your siblings and serving Mom in the home. We couldn't have done it without you!

Cyndy, for once again giving so much of your time to help us communicate our hearts in an understandable way. Both your talents and your friendship are much appreciated.

Ted, for your last-minute availability and very helpful comments on the manuscript (Matthew 16:28!).

Nora and Patsy, for your friendship and support expressed in phone calls, prayers, cards, meals and offers to help with the children. Thanks for being there for us!

The excellent people of Fairfax Covenant Church, for supporting us in prayer and for being living testimonies of the principles in this book. It is our privilege to serve you!

Contents

1 Expanding Your Vision for Parenthood   15
2 Fashioning Young Arrows   23
3 The American Family in Crisis   36
4 Are Christian Families Exempt?   55
5 Shaping Their Concept of God   68
6 Respect: A Crucial Foundation   84
7 Training Children to Become Responsible   99
8 Fostering a Responsive Heart   116
9 Seeing Results Through Discipline that Works 129
10 Parenting and the Grace of God   145
11 Keys to Motivating Children Successfully   159
12 A Mother's Influence   174
13 Modeling the Fatherhood of God   185
14 Faith for the Adolescent Years   206
15 Leading Your Children to the Lord   230

Preface

"No civilization has suffered the loss of two successive generations and survived. We've already lost one."

This warning from Chuck Colson, former White House aide and founder of Prison Fellowship, alerts today's parents to the critical hour in which we live. Today's young people are being lost in record numbers to substance abuse, violent crime, suicide and sexually transmitted diseases.

As Christian parents, we may hear of such tragedies and sigh with relief. "I'm so glad I don't have to worry about anything like that happening to my children." Surely our children's church involvement and their avoidance of peers who could influence them negatively protect our families from such heartache.

Thankfully, our commitment to our children and our desire to rear them according to biblical principles may indeed protect them from the kind of lifestyle that leads to such tragic conclusions. The possibility of our children's being lost to worldly values and self-gratification, however, is real. Recent surveys suggest that church involvement alone makes little difference in the daily lives and moral values of young people. One well-publicized survey, conducted by

Wheaton College and Campus Crusade for Christ, revealed less than a ten percent difference between the morality of churched and non-churched students. "It seems obvious," comments Dr. Robert Laurent in his book *Keeping Your Teen in Touch with God*, "that the Gospel of Jesus Christ is making little difference in the lives of many teenagers."

This is the potential heartbreak of today's generation of Christian parents and their children. Few things could hurt us more than seeing our children drift apathetically from their Christian upbringing into selfish pursuits and moral compromise.

Do you long for your children to experience the kind of relationship with the Lord that equips them to be a light to their generation—a "city on a hill" that cannot be hidden? Do you want them to discover and fulfill God's unique plan for their lives? Are you content with their attendance at church, or do you want to see them become passionately involved in the mission of God for their generation?

Such goals will not be reached by a halfhearted commitment to parenthood, over-delegating the spiritual training of our children to others. Rather, we must fully embrace our God-given responsibility to disciple our children into such a lifestyle.

Christian leader and author Arthur Wallis once said, "If you would do the best with your life, find out what God is doing in your generation and fling yourself into it." As a parent, you have been entrusted with the privilege of rearing your children to do just this. Rather than watch them prepare to fling themselves into self-fulfillment, you can be used by God to cultivate in them a desire to know Jesus Christ and discover His call on their lives.

As with most married couples, Sheree and I are nearly opposite in personality. We usually approach situations from very different perspectives. We have our share of disagreements over which of us misplaced the car keys or whether we should make a certain purchase. Over the thirteen years we've been parents, however, we have begun to learn the critical importance of being "on the same page" regarding childrearing.

No, we don't always agree on every detail of training, instructing and disciplining our children. We do, however, share a common burden each to do our part to see our children become strong in character and enjoy a vital relationship with Jesus Christ. Parenting has provided the common ground for our different personalities and perspectives to complement and stimulate one another.

Implementing our goals for our children is difficult at times, and we are both learning to recognize and appreciate the unique strengths the other brings to parenting. Like most Christian couples, we recognize our deep need for one another.

If you are a single parent, be patient with our frequent references to family life with both father and mother. We trust you will glean insights that will assist and encourage you.

Whether you are single or married, parenting children who will be radical followers of God is a goal we are sure you aspire to. Our prayer is that this book will assist you to that end.

1
Expanding Your Vision for Parenthood

Benny

One fall evening several years ago, Joshua, then five, joined Sheree and me as we watched a televised evangelistic crusade from the Philippines. The speaker was making a moving appeal for individuals to give their lives to see the Gospel preached through the earth. As people made their way to the platform to give themselves to God for this purpose, we glanced at Joshua. He was watching the scene intently, tears forming in his eyes.

I wondered if we should interrupt this moment with a question. From a very young age Joshua, seeing people respond to the Gospel, had responded similarly, especially since he had prayed to "make Jesus boss of his life." I wanted to know what was happening in our son's heart.

"Look at all those people responding to the message," I commented. "What do you think about that?" Just then the evangelist looked into the camera to appeal directly to his viewers. His plea for us to consider going into the world to preach the Gospel kept Joshua's attention. Then he turned to give me a hug.

"I want to go and help people know about Jesus," he said, the tears now falling down his cheeks.

It was one of those holy moments. I knew instinctively that the way we responded was critical. I didn't want to make too much or too little of what Joshua was feeling. So I simply held him, told him what a sweet, responsive boy he was and how pleased Jesus was by his compassion.

Again the speaker appealed to his television audience. "God is calling some of you to spread the Gospel in foreign lands. Pray with me now and consecrate yourself, along with those who have responded here in Manila, to Him." As he prayed, Sheree explained the speaker's words in a way our five-year-old could understand.

As soon as the prayer was completed, Joshua looked up and asked if he was too little to ask Jesus to let him share the Gospel. I assured him no one was too young to respond to a call to share the love of God with others. And when he asked if I could pray the way the speaker did, we asked Jesus together to prepare Joshua to share the Good News with those who needed to hear it, especially those in foreign lands.

"Now I know what I want to be when I grow up," he declared as we all wiped the tears from our eyes. "I want to be an evangelist."

In reflecting over the next few years on this memorable incident, Sheree and I valued Joshua's response to what he heard more than his expressed desire to become an evangelist. We wondered if and how long this desire would continue before he decided to become a pilot or carpenter or professional athlete—professions we were glad to help him achieve if he desired.

This experience also prompted questions of just how early in life God may place prophetic desires in our children's hearts of their eventual call. How could we prepare them for whatever God has in store? When His will becomes clear—whether it is for them to evangelize in foreign lands or to teach math to high school students as a loving role model—we want to have done our parts to train them to embrace God's will for their lives. Doing this requires that we teach our children to hunger for an intimate relationship with God.

Challenged as to how we could prepare Joshua for usefulness to God, Sheree and I stumbled onto an answer when he was twelve. Joshua had tried over the years to convince several of the neighborhood children to give their hearts to Jesus. He had organized the "Phillips Evangelism Club" to distribute Gospel tracts. He and a friend had each asked for music lessons so they could organize a band to do evangelistic concerts in their teenage years. All this "practice," he explained, would help prepare him to become an evangelist someday.

Were Joshua's desires for ministry a natural response to being a pastor's son? Possibly. Yet Sheree and I were eager to cooperate with his aspirations, knowing that some of the childhood dreams we ourselves had experienced had turned out to be God's promptings in our own young hearts.

Now, seven years after Joshua's prayer of commitment in front of the television set, we were all in the van running errands. Jaime asked her siblings what they wanted to be when they grew up.

"I want to sing to children and tell them stories from the Bible," said then-five-year-old Jesse, apparently remembering a recent concert for the children of our church.

"I want to be a waitress until I become a mommy and have lots of children," said Jaime.

"I know what I want to be," added three-year-old Joey. "I want to be a horse!"

After we all stopped laughing, Jaime asked Josh for his response.

"I still want to be an evangelist," he responded, "but I know I have a lot to work on before that can happen."

Joshua was apparently thinking about conversations we had had recently about areas in his character that needed work. His pre-adolescent years had shown us some tendencies toward contention and arrogance. Some of what was happening in him, we knew, was developmental for his age. Yet we were unwilling to simply accept as part of the growing-up process his temptation to argue, to blame his siblings for things he was responsible for, or to hesitate to admit freely when he was wrong. Rather, we had chosen to address these tendencies, lovingly and consistently, as unacceptable to us and displeasing to God. These were the days in which Joshua's understanding of God's nature were being critically shaped.

"You know, Josh," I said now, "character development really is essential in fulfilling whatever God calls you to. His acceptance of you has nothing to do with either your positive or your negative qualities. But those negative qualities will only slow you down in becoming a man God can use."

Once again tears welled up in his eyes. "Are you saying that the reason you've been pointing so many things out to me lately is because you're trying to help prepare me for my future?"

"Yes, son. One of Mom's and my biggest goals in life is to help you become the mature man God wants you to be—and that *you* want to be."

"Wow," he said softly. "Thanks, Mom and Dad."

That day the light went on in our hearts as well. Suddenly we, too, had a revelation of how we could practically prepare our children to obey and love God. Bible stories, excellent children's ministry on Sundays, friendships with other well-mannered children, even family worship times, are not the primary keys to developing a heart for God in our children. The best path to ensure their hunger for God is building foundational character qualities in their lives and providing an inspiring model for them to follow.

Every Christian parent longs to see his or her children grow in devotion to God and in resistance to worldly temptation. Many of today's parents were reared in churchgoing homes only to reject our parents' "religion" during adolescence. Some of us reacted to legalism. Others stumbled over those professing to love God while living compromising lifestyles. Still others rebelled against Christianity simply because we desired to taste the pleasures of sin that the church prohibited.

How we yearn now to see our children avoid the heartache that walking in compromise brings! Yet selfishness or ignorance often causes us parents to choose the easy way to silence our fears that they will drift away from God.

What is the "easy" way? Every parent is tempted to delegate to others prematurely or unwisely the responsibility of leading our children spiritually. After all, we can now provide Christian videos to replace unwholesome television programs. Christian bookstores provide books, devotional material, music and lots of other helpful resources. Churches appeal increasingly to a generation of parents for whom an active children's ministry is a priority. Christian schools are opening at an average of one per day with activities and curriculum designed to rival those of the public schools.

Today's generation of parents, many of them baby boomers, is the largest and best-educated generation in history. For the most part, we are serious about parenting. As

Christians we have an intense desire to provide the best in everything for our children. Yet even those of us who take seriously our responsibility to care for our children spiritually can take the easy way. We may assume that providing regular family devotions, reading age-appropriate Bible stories and not letting them play with the boy down the street who uses vulgar language are the best ways to encourage our children's relationship with the Lord.

To be sure, all these things help. Sheree and I have felt the frustration of doing all this, yet wondered if there isn't a way to deal more directly with the day-to-day challenges, such as when the children bicker over who will sit in the front seat of the car while running errands with Daddy. As a pastor I have seen many heartbroken parents experience the shock of seeing their teenage children reared in the church reject God or become involved in drugs or premarital sex.

The "easy" things shouldn't necessarily be disregarded. They should simply be viewed as supplements to the more important ways we can cultivate a heart for God in our children. It is easy to read them Bible stories. It is difficult and time-consuming to help them spot and overcome selfishness, pride or worldliness—traits that will ultimately rob them of passion for God and His Church.

We can learn a lesson from the principle outlined in 1 Corinthians 15:46 (although the context of this verse doesn't relate to our subject), in which Paul speaks of the "natural" coming before the "spiritual." In fostering love for God in our children, we must not minimize the importance of the natural—qualities like respect, courage, diligence and unselfishness needed for functioning in everyday circumstances, and which help provide the necessary foundation for the spiritual to develop.

God wants an army of young people who will stand alone

against worldly temptations and be a prophetic voice to their generation. This will not happen merely by providing wholesome entertainment and Christian reading material. It will come primarily when parents take seriously their responsibility to rear spiritually mature children—those who have been trained to be responsive, obedient and ripe for usefulness to God.

A halfhearted attempt to cultivate our children's spiritual development will lead to young people with halfhearted commitment to God. As parents, we must pay whatever price required to devote ourselves to biblical principles of child-rearing. It is time to refuse the self-absorption that our career, relationships and personal struggles demand from us. For while we are distracted by these things, our children may drift slowly out of the church and into the world.

The principles we will share in the following pages are for those who agree with author Gordon MacDonald's view of parenting as a "preoccupying way of life." Your success will require availability to your children unmatched by the average parent in our society. You will be challenged to re-evaluate your relationship with God and overcome any hindrances to becoming the kind of model your children can follow. Our goal is to motivate you to make whatever dramatic changes are necessary in your schedule, attitude and character to make a commitment to your children that few parents are willing to make.

Your children need you, your time, your affection, your attention, your guidance. The price is high, but what greater joy could there be in this life than seeing them enjoy a fervent relationship with Jesus Christ that permeates every area of their lives?

Every generation of children needs this kind of parental commitment. Yet the challenges and temptations young people face today issue a particularly urgent call for Christian parents willing to resist the self-gratifying spirit of our culture to devote themselves to the high calling of parenthood.

My wife and I have been privileged with the assignment of raising six children to know and serve Jesus Christ. We have been blessed with some successes. We have had to persevere through challenges. Our children have shown encouraging signs of deep love for God as we watch them worship on Sunday mornings. Yet they are normal, active youngsters who will be outside playing together—and, yes, arguing together—that very afternoon. Spending their childhoods quoting passages from Zephaniah and discussing Calvinism versus Arminianism is not our goal for them. Every Christian parent's goal is to see his or her child enjoy an intimate relationship with the Lord and be used to bring His Kingdom into others' lives.

Proverbs 29:18 warns that without a vision the people will wander aimlessly. You may be among those parents who lack focus and direction for rearing your children. You may be fearful of your children's adolescent years. You may feel overwhelmed by the awesome challenges. Or you may simply want help to cope with an uncooperative, disrespectful toddler. Allowing God to give you a fresh vision for child-rearing—goals, strategy and faith for results—can give parenting new meaning and provide answers to your questions.

Sheree and I would like to share from our experiences how you can foster your children's hearts for Jesus Christ. We have tried the easy way at times and seen minimal results. Choosing the more difficult way of helping our children conform to the image of the One who longs to have a relationship with them has produced in us faith for their future. We hope the insights we share will help you in the task of raising your children to hunger for God.

Unless, of course, one of them grows up to be a horse!

2
Fashioning Young Arrows

Benny

Many of today's Christian baby boom parents—those born in the post-war years of 1946 to 1964—are facing unique spiritual challenges with their children.

Many became Christians during the Jesus movement of the late '60s and early '70s when tens of thousands of young people came out of the world and into the Church. They were a drug-using, insecure, rebellious generation disillusioned with the religion they had grown up with, which seemed to have little effect on people's lives.

In my own high school, the most unlikely individuals grew interested in reading the Bible. The captain of the football team became a Christian and started a Bible study. Within months, dozens of us met weekly to sit cross-legged on the basement floor of a local church building with guitars and Bibles in hand—quite a change for many of us who had had a penchant for troublemaking, myself included. We sang simple choruses, prayed aloud for the first time in our lives, read

Scripture passages we didn't really understand, and found a relationship with Jesus Christ that brought meaning and purpose into our lives. Those who had become Christians just weeks before taught new converts. Christian singing groups like "The Second Chapter of Acts" replaced the music that once blared from our eight-track car stereos.

For Sheree and me, much of our courtship revolved around attending those meetings, spending time with friends to discuss the Bible, and church activities. Many of our friends committed their lives to the Lord. Christianity became a preoccupying way of life. Although we had both been raised in evangelical churches and had responded early to the Gospel, our relationships with the Lord had never had such meaning.

And by God's grace, Sheree and I escaped the tragic outcome of many of our peers who ended up leaving Jesus behind. Of the hundreds from our school who committed themselves to the Lord, only a handful are walking with God today. But most of us, including those who have maintained our relationship with Him, are now married with children fast approaching their teenage years. And nothing is quite so frightening as anticipating our children's journey through adolescence without a relationship with the Lord.

Most of us are concerned about forcing our Christianity on our children the way we felt our parents' religion was forced on us. But we are more concerned about the consequences of letting them simply drift their own way. We long for them to avoid the snares of drugs, premarital sex, peer pressure and selling out for the acceptance of others. We don't want them to carry the baggage that youthful sin brings into adulthood.

How can we cause our children to long to know God? What can we do to cultivate in them the kind of radical commitment to Jesus Christ that makes it easy to flee relationships and activities that would compromise their walk with Him? How can we teach them to say no to temptation and maintain godly standards, especially when we are not around to hold them accountable? And how do we motivate them to influence others for the Kingdom of God rather than be influenced by others to sin?

We will discuss many possible answers to these critical questions in later chapters, but two important principles lay the foundation for the practical solutions to come.

First, we must realize that *God has a unique purpose for our children's generation.* Doesn't God feel this way about every generation? Every parent would like to believe that God wants to use his or her children in a special way. But what could be distinctive about any particular plan?

I had a similar response when I began to ponder this first foundational principle. In preparation for teaching a series called "Parenting: From Survival to Success," I decided to research some biblical insights on the subject. My study began in Psalm 127:3–5:

> Sons are a heritage from the Lord, children a reward from him. Like arrows in the hands of a warrior are sons born in one's youth. Blessed is the man whose quiver is full of them. They will not be put to shame when they contend with their enemies in the gate.

We can see from this passage that God's view of children is profoundly different from ours. He sees our children as battle instruments against our enemy, Satan. An arrow is a weapon with great potential. A young, sharp arrow entrusted to faithful parents is a tremendous threat to our foe. So what must well-trained, spiritually mature, boldly courageous young people be? More like what one believer calls heat-seeking missiles!

Our responsibility as parents is like that of the arrow-maker. We take a piece of wood and invest delicate, hard work, fashioning it into an arrow. We make it straight and strong. We take whatever painstaking effort is necessary to whittle it carefully and precisely. No detail is too small. (Branches quickly collected and minimally prepared will not hit the target and spare our lives.) At last, the weapon we have been designing methodically is ready to be launched against the enemy. A well-made, well-aimed arrow finds its mark swiftly and accurately.

King David understood God's heart for children to be used to advance His Kingdom and thwart Satan's purposes. In Psalm 8:2 David declared that "from the lips of children and infants you have ordained praise because of your enemies, to silence the foe and the avenger." What an awesome privilege we have as parents! God has equipped us through our children with forces that can destroy Satan's plans for evil in the earth.

How, then, does the next generation hold a unique part in God's agenda? I certainly don't have all answers, but biblical history suggests there is a prophetic call on our children's lives.

Consider what happened at two crucial times in Jewish history—the time of Moses and the time of Jesus. Both were born at critical times for unique reasons. Moses was called to lead his people from captivity in Egypt to the land of God's promise. Jesus, of course, was the Messiah—the One to be the ransom for man's sin.

The book of Exodus begins with the circumstances surrounding Moses' birth in Egypt. As God had promised Abraham, the Israelites had grown too numerous to count.

Pharaoh decided that they could be a threat, so he placed them under slavery. Still they multiplied, until he ordered all baby boys born to Hebrew women to be killed (Exodus 1:16). Moses' mother hid him in a basket on the river, hoping someone would rescue him from potential slaughter. God spared Moses' life, allowed him to be reared by Pharaoh's daughter and raised him up to lead his people out of slavery.

Thousands of years later, history repeated itself. When King Herod was unable to find the baby who had been born "king of the Jews," he ordered that all boys under age two be killed (Matthew 2:16). An angel warned Joseph in a dream to flee to Egypt. Later the family returned to Nazareth and Jesus grew in wisdom and truth, fulfilled His mission to die in our place, rose from the grave, and now sits at the right hand of God—God's triumphant battle against Satan.

Two thousand years later, history has repeated itself once again. In January 1973, while the Church was sleeping unaware, the highest court in our nation ruled it lawful to slaughter innocent children. Unfortunately, it was impossible for concerned people to hide them or sneak away with them in the night. The little ones would be slaughtered in their mothers' wombs. At this writing, eighteen years later, 26 million babies have died through abortion.

Coincidence or design? When I first heard a believer share this remarkable parallel, I was struck with the prophetic application it suggests. Could it be that, just as with Moses and Jesus, Satan has become aware of the deliverance God intends to bring to our society, not through one man, but through a generation of children who will be "mighty in the land" (Psalm 112:2)—ones who will stand against the tide of secularism and sacrifice all to see the nations reached for the Gospel, and thus hasten Jesus' return (2 Peter 3:11–12)?

What a thrilling thought! Rather than our children being

used by the enemy to spread the ills in our society, God wants them to become a counterculture to turn the hearts of their peers to the God who longs to fellowship with and use them. This presents to us, as those who have been entrusted with our children's training and discipleship, an awesome challenge.

Job 8:8-13 gives us a sobering picture of this challenge:

> Ask the former generations and find out what their fathers learned, for we were born only yesterday and know nothing, and our days on earth are but a shadow. Will they not instruct you and tell you? Will they not bring forth words from their understanding? Can papyrus grow tall where there is no marsh? Can reeds thrive without water? While still growing and uncut, they wither more quickly than grass. Such is the destiny of all who forget God.

Today's young parents are beginning to realize that the childrearing methods and values of previous generations are not to be so quickly disregarded. The permissive, undisciplined approach championed in the late 1950s and '60s is causing some to fear for their children's spiritual condition. Yet parents today are often ill-equipped to return to more traditional ways of training them.

The analogy in Job 8 that papyrus can't grow "where there is no marsh" and that reeds won't "thrive without water" warns us that it is fruitless to look to untried ways of raising our children, even though our natural minds see good in them. Childrearing methods must have a strong biblical foundation to warrant our confidence. Much of the advice of recent decades is rooted in the humanistic philosophies so prevalent in society (mankind is basically good; one path to truth is as good as another; etc.). Disregarding timeless biblical principles will only bring about what we fear: children who reject the Lord and "wither more quickly than grass."

What are some practical ways we can begin to fashion these arrows for God's arsenal, to nurture these "reeds" and do our part to see that they are well-watered and strong?

First, we must change our perspective on parenting. Getting caught up in the daily responsibilities of parenthood can prevent us from sustaining an eternal perspective on our ministry to our children. Without a long-term vision for their future, we will lose our passion to excel in example, discipline and instruction and are left to muddle through the weeks and years simply hoping they will "turn out O.K." Our responsibilities become mechanical and we can easily lose heart when we encounter challenges in discipline or our children's spiritual disinterest. By maintaining an "arrowmaker's mentality," on the other hand, we have a heightened sense of motivation, creativity and perseverance in the tasks of parenting. Even daily happenings become opportunities to sharpen our future weapons further against the enemy.

Second, we must cultivate a spiritually active atmosphere in our homes. Praying before meals and reading bedtime Bible stories alone will do little to nurture spiritually mature young people. Seeing our children as a generation of arrows, on the other hand, will motivate us to invite them to join us in praying for people and family decisions when appropriate, by discerning their readiness for salvation and for exercising spiritual gifts, by encouraging them to share the Gospel with their friends, and by praying regularly that they have a growing hunger for God.

Third, we must develop a loyal spirit in our children. When Christianity is mocked on every side and young people are tempted far beyond what today's parents faced at their age, it is critical that we train our children to be loyal to biblical standards, values and convictions. Many Christian parents have watched their teenagers, unable to stand alone against the pressure, spurn their upbringing in the face of peer influence and worldly seduction. Sheree and I will offer suggestions about how to develop a loyal spirit in your children in a later chapter.

Once Christian parents catch a glimpse of the unique call God may have on our children's generation—and this is the second foundational principle for parenting—we can then *cultivate the faith necessary to excel in parenting*. Sheree and I have found it easier to embrace and actually enjoy our responsibilities as parents since we have acquired a better glimpse of what is at stake for our children. Faith makes investing the hard work necessary to get the results we desire more than worth the effort.

Several years ago Sheree came across the idea of getting what an author called "faith pictures" for our children. Mike Phillips in his book *Blueprint for Raising a Child* suggested that by studying our children early to discern their strengths and weaknesses, we can get a glimpse of the kind of person God wants each to become.

Since then, Sheree and I have enjoyed viewing our children in this way. We have seen that Joshua's desire for people to know Jesus might reveal the heart of a budding evangelist. We have wondered if Jesse's emotional sensitivity might be used by God someday in counseling or pastoring. We have seen that Jaime's bent toward expressive and enthusiastic worship could be excellent preparation for her becoming a worship leader. Each of our children displays qualities that produce these "faith pictures" in our minds and help us to work on any negative qualities that could prohibit their development. We hold our thoughts for their future lightly until confirmation of God's plans for them; but meanwhile, we benefit from looking beyond today into our children's future to help us with the task of training them for it.

Although the specifics are yet unclear, one faith picture we have for each child is to see him or her continue to grow in love for and devotion to God. Our deepest passion in life is to create in each an insatiable desire to follow Jesus Christ down whatever road He may lead. We long for each one to be among the generation of radical seekers of God (Psalm 24:3–6).

The most important of the many ways parents can help to fulfill this desire is simple: We must cultivate our own relationship with the Lord and then share it with our children. Our generation resisted religious forms and church attendance that made little difference the rest of the week. Why would our children react any differently?

New Testament Christianity, on the other hand, was not characterized primarily by meetings and rituals. It was characterized by people who loved God passionately and unashamedly. They were eager to share their faith with others, and they lived out their faith in a community lifestyle. No, they didn't create a commune and begin sharing toothbrushes, but they shared meals, helped to meet one another's practical needs and experienced the benefits of unselfish servanthood (see Acts 2:42–47; 4:32–37).

Sheree and I have sought to emulate this New Testament pattern with the church God has privileged us to serve. Our members enjoy helping one another pack, move and set up in a new home. Singles in our midst babysit for couples so they can have a night out together or attend a couples' function in the church. The ladies regularly provide more than a week of dinners for mothers just home with their new babies. Our church calendar is full of hospitalities, meetings for various age groups, outings for singles, parties for teenagers, and other good excuses for us to be together as a "family."

Our children benefit from being part of our community lifestyle. They help prepare meals. They serve at our hospitalities. They join in our prayers for a sick child in the church and are likely to follow up with a note to the child or inquire about how that child is doing. We fill them in on exciting news of God's provision or the blessing of someone we know and they join us in praise and thanksgiving.

The following verses help to underscore the importance of our sharing the goodness of God with our children:

Even when I am old and gray, do not forsake me, O God, till I declare your power to the next generation, your might to all who are to come.   Psalm 71:18

I will open my mouth in parables, I will utter things hidden from of old—things we have heard and known, things our fathers have told us. We will not hide them from their children; we will tell the next generation the praiseworthy deeds of the Lord, his power, and the wonders he has done.   Psalm 78:2–4

Walk about Zion [i.e., the people of God], go around her, count her towers, consider well her ramparts, view her citadels, that you may tell of them to the next generation.   Psalm 48:12–13

These commandments that I give you today are to be upon your hearts. Impress them on your children. Talk about them when you sit at home and when you walk along the road, when you lie down and when you get up.   Deuteronomy 6:6–7

My own ability to tell my children about the power, provision and love of God requires that I first experience these things on a deeply personal level. Communicating spiritual information to them will not impress them nearly as much as imparting my heart to them. Parents whose relationship with the Lord is characterized by regular times of worship, daily dependence on Him, prayer and fasting (hold the applause), enthusiastic praise, a lifestyle of integrity and service to others, and childlike excitement over the deeds of the Lord will inspire their children to want to know such a God.

Several years ago when Joshua was seven, he took it upon himself to set his alarm for an early hour. After several days I began to notice this ritual and learned that Josh had decided to start getting up early to pray, just like Daddy. This, he said, made him "feel like a man." Times like this have deepened my faith that my children will continue to grow in love for God. Although Josh is not yet consistent in early morning prayer, this incident was among the first signs of his self-initiated pursuit of a relationship with the Lord. *(Lord, help me to become a consistent example to him!)*

Jesus said that faith as small as a mustard seed could move a mountain (Mark 4:30–32). Seeing our children become spiritually mature and zealous to advance God's Kingdom requires faith to move the mountain of worldliness that would steal their fervor for Him.

Parenting has taken on new meaning for me as I come to understand that true faith is active, not passive. "Faith without deeds is useless," James warns (2:20). Having faith for my own children's spiritual development is not expressed merely by praying for them regularly. Nor is it rooted in naïve hope that allows them to go their own way because sooner or later they will "return to the fold." Rather, true faith is confidence in biblical principles of childrearing that expresses itself in *actively* teaching, disciplining and training them every day.

With faith, the regular activities of parenting take on long-term significance. Training children to clean their rooms builds the responsible attitudes they will need later—on the job and at home. Teaching them to relate to others respectfully creates an environment of unselfishness in the home. Keeping promises to them sets an example for them to be men and women of their word in years to come.

When mixed with patience, faith also helps us to persevere through challenging seasons of our children's spiritual apathy or their return to wrong attitudes we thought they had overcome. Faith reminds us not to give in to unnecessary fear, knowing that they experience seasons of slow and rapid character growth just as we do. It also motivates us to deal consistently and lovingly with areas in their lives that need our correction and instruction without expecting immediate fruit from our labor.

Faith also guards our hearts when others ridicule us for the way we are raising our children. When relatives and friends question our decisions concerning our children's exposure to various people or activities, we can be humbly confident in articulating our convictions. When we are accused of "sheltering our children from the real world" because we dissociate them from a peer who is influencing them negatively or because we monitor what they watch on television, we can resist the temptation to feel insecure and apologetic. Faith allows us to stand our ground without arrogance and guards us from comparing our childrearing standards to those of others who do not share our commitment to biblical values.

Sheree and I don't have all the answers for readying our young arrows for battle; we continue to learn from more experienced parents. But faith rises in my heart for this generation that Satan has attempted to slaughter. Yes, my faith wanes at times, but then it bounces back to affirm that God indeed wants to use us as parents to participate in the task of fashioning our children as weapons to advance His Kingdom.

How can we do this? What are some of the obstacles we face? With faith in our hearts, let's begin to examine some helpful aspects to equip us for the job!

3
The American Family in Crisis

Benny

Even the most casual observer would not dispute that the American family is in danger. Society has rejected and now actively opposes traditional standards for family living that were practiced only decades ago.

For its part, our culture has fallen prey to the deception of self-gratification and secularism. The divorce rate in our nation is the highest in the world at 46%, having risen an astounding 300 percent in the past 25 years. Forty percent of all children in this country will face, by their eighteenth birthday, the heartache of their parents' divorce. Christian family counselor and author Dr. James Dobson states that a mere seven percent of families are defined as "traditional"— a working father and homemaking mother with their natural children. The effects of these departures from historical and biblical norms on children is only just beginning to be seen. In fact, *Time* magazine observed in a report on "The Changing Family" (special issue on women, fall 1990): "Today's parents are raising children in ways that little resemble their own youth. The question that haunts them: Will the kids be all right?"

The Washington Times (October 31, 1989) cited recent findings by the Rockford Institute and the Family Research Council, which have concluded that divorce carries some significant effects on children. Children of divorce are twenty times more likely to be poor, "more likely than others to need psychiatric care and to run afoul of the law," and more likely to have a higher frequency of illnesses.

The social upheaval of recent decades, it seems, has done more to shake the family than we could ever have realized. Children can no longer rely on the security of growing up in a stable environment.

The stage is set for the emergence of righteous, uncompromising parents willing to pay the price to build their families securely upon biblical principles. If we don't accept the challenge, more may be at stake than we imagine. Christian leader Charles Simpson aptly notes that "any plans that Satan has to destroy society might first begin with the family. That was his strategy in the garden, and in the fall of every successive society. According to the Bible, all human suffering can be traced to failure in the first [family]. It is easily demonstrated that family failures are still the leading causes of suffering." Witness, as just one example, the enormity of the current recovery movement, with its roots in the so-called dysfunctional family.

Only as we are successful in equipping ourselves to battle the forces fighting our families can we create an environment that will cause our children to want to know the God we serve.

Let's look, then, at six primary onslaughts against the family.

Selfishness

Most of today's parents were reared in the me-centered individualism of the '60s and '70s. Our own parents, having faced the challenges of Depression and war, sought to provide for us in ways they had not been able to enjoy. Unfortunately, many of us took advantage of their well-meaning desire by becoming ungrateful and materialistic—not in the '60s, maybe, but certainly since then. The media has fed our self-awareness by convincing us that we "deserve a break" at McDonalds; that we are "worth" the extra money for Preference hair color; that we should "grab for all the gusto" we can get in life.

The consequences of this attitude are evident in the American family. Couples give up on their marriages too quickly without weighing the devastating long-term challenges they and their children will face. Mothers return to the work force soon after giving birth, not only to help make ends meet, but sometimes because they enjoy the material benefits of the larger home, extra car or spending money. Men absorb themselves in moving up the corporate ladder without noticing how their wives and children are suffering from their lack of love, availability and involvement.

Even Christian parents who haven't given in to these pressures can be deceived into thinking selfishness is not a problem. Sheree and I have seen the subtle effects of self-absorption in our own family life.

Parenting requires a level of unselfishness that few are prepared for. Newborns are notorious for crying during dinner, wanting to be fed at the supermarket, and soiling their freshly changed clothes when we're already running late on Sunday morning. Toddlers wet their training pants in line at department stores and practice writing their names on the bedroom walls. Teenagers forget to tell you they have basketball practice until fifteen minutes beforehand, and they remind you they are scheduled to use the car on the night you planned a romantic dinner together out.

It is amazing how such seemingly insignificant happenings can surface a selfish reaction—speaking harshly to our children, impatience, irritation and frustration—all natural but nevertheless selfish reactions to being inconvenienced by the demands and responsibilities of parenthood.

Paul's exhortation in Philippians 2:3–4 is especially appropriate in relating to our children: "Do nothing out of selfish ambition . . . but in humility consider others better than yourselves. Each of you should look not only to your own interests, but also to the interests of others."

Unselfish availability to our children's needs does not require dropping everything to serve their every demand. They too must learn to apply this important verse to their lives. To deal radically with selfishness, however, helps us to enjoy and embrace the awesome privileges of raising young lives for God.

I once heard it said that pressure introduces a man to himself. Selfishness in my own life has been the greatest factor to introduce me to hindrances to effective fatherhood. Too often I fight the temptation to preoccupation with my adult responsibilities. I am more eager at the dinner table to talk about my own day than to ask the children about theirs. On those occasions when Sheree's absence gives me full responsibility for the children, I am often too eager for her to return to relieve me of diapers, sibling arguments, straightening and restraightening the kitchen and answering questions like "What holds the clouds up?"

Normal adult attitudes? Maybe. Yet such seemingly small seeds of selfishness develop potentially dangerous roots that thwart healthy parent-child relationships.

Societal Bias Against the Family

A second force fighting the family is a current societal bias that minimizes the value of the family. My own family experiences certain aspects of this regularly.

Grocery shopping or going out to a restaurant together is quite a feat for us. Since we have six children in tow, hardly anyone resists the temptation to stare, count heads or offer the incredulous "Are they all yours?" question. At our affirmative response, most people either smile or politely respond with something like, "Boy, I hardly made it through two!"

Some are warmly encouraging, especially older folks who have large families and are now enjoying grandchildren.

Others, however, have voiced their apparent prejudice against "too many" children. We have received our share of comments like, "Better you than me," "Haven't you figured out how they get here yet?" or, "Don't you know this world's overpopulated?" We don't resent such attitudes. Rather, we realize that apart from having God's heart on parenting we could be tempted to share similar philosophies.

After our second child was born we were the ideal American family with a son and a daughter. We fit into a compact car, could eat out inexpensively and survived in the mall, each of us holding one child's hand. I was especially content with our family and Sheree was happy with the reprieve from colic and night feedings.

Then, just as Jaime was potty-trained and the crib was stored safely in the attic, a strange thing happened. Sheree started talking about having another baby. In our discussions we weighed the pros and cons of another child. And over the months I began to see an unsettling pattern in my reasons for limiting our family to four. Most seemed to have been influenced by secular reasoning. Our peers were having a national average of 1.8 children. We would need a larger car. College tuition rates would be hard enough to come up with for two. We could certainly provide more for the two children we had if we didn't have any more. In the long run, our lives would be more comfortable if things stayed as they were.

As Christians, I realized, we should not base our decisions on what anyone thinks, but rather on God's principles. And although I wanted to consider the economic and practical factors of determining our family's size, I knew that only prayer and studying what the Bible had to say about children would bring the answers I needed. (I have already shared some of these answers, and will share more in the chapters ahead.)

Since then, with each child God has given us has come the grace to accept him or her joyfully as a divinely ordained addition to our family. Over time, despite the questions I had about how adding another child would stretch us, I realized that the challenges were opportunities to grow in faith toward God. As the years have passed and I experience the joy of seeing our six children grow, I am all the more grateful for the work the Lord has done in me.

This process has also helped me better understand the anxieties and misconceptions others have about parenthood. Sheree and I were naïvely unaware of the tremendous responsibilities involved in raising children. Now we are deeply concerned about the influence a wrong perspective on parenting has exerted on our society. Currently, 1.6 million children are aborted every year while thousands of loving couples wait for years on adoption lists. More and more couples are choosing not to have children in order to maintain a standard of living to which they have grown accustomed. (The number of children per family in our Washington, D.C., suburb is currently 0.7.)

Many parents view children as an expense, an interruption in the wife's career, a tolerable accommodation of relatives who want nieces or grandchildren. Still others abdicate their parental responsibility so they can provide more "things" for the family, and deprive their children of parental bonding by delegating childrearing to others.

I am not suggesting that everyone have a large family. Nor am I insensitive to the growing number of single parents (some 9.3 million of them) facing the consequences of divorce or sexual involvement outside of marriage, to whom the Church is privileged and responsible to minister. I simply offer the admonition Sheree and I heard in a new way nearly a decade ago during our decision-making process about family size:

> Therefore, I urge you, brothers, in view of God's mercy, to offer your bodies as living sacrifices, holy and pleasing to God—which is your spiritual worship. Do not conform any longer to the pattern of this world, but be transformed by the renewing of your mind. Then you will be able to test and approve what God's will is—his good, pleasing and perfect will.   Romans 12:1–2

Alternative Authorities

A third force in our society fighting the family is the growing number of "experts" telling us how to raise our children. Because most of today's parents are untrained for the responsibility, it is important to admit our need for instruction, especially from those of previous generations. As Christians, however, we must exercise discernment over whose advice we accept. Nor should we try the newest method of childrearing advocated in bookstores or on talk shows without seeing first how it lines up with God's Word.

Unfortunately, these other methods may also be imposed by default as care of our children is increasingly delegated to others. Not only (as we have already discussed) are mothers leaving their infants and toddlers to return to work, but couples are enrolling toddlers in "enrichment" programs and pre-schools as soon as possible. Many states are advocating earlier mandatory school entrance requirements even though studies show that many youngsters are unable to learn in a structured environment until age ten. More experts are recommending values and sex education programs in the public schools. Then there are extracurricular activities like ballet, sports or Scouts, good in themselves, but which limit the time families spend together. And let's not forget the massive encroachment of television on family time as well as values.

In his book *The Hurried Child*, David Elkind educates us as to another pressure on young children. Many children in our society are so "hurried" from one activity to another, he suggests, that they feel stress and become insecure. "A latch-key child, for example, is hurried because he or she is expected to cope with a difficult situation being home alone for extended periods of time. A child who has to go to a babysitter and then a daycare center and then a babysitter again is hurried because the child has to make too many adaptations in a small period of time."

What a striking contrast with just a century ago when home was the center of family life! Prior to the Industrial Revolution, according to Penelope Leach, author of *Your Baby and Child*, children spent the majority of their time with the families. There, of course, they would have been prepared for their future roles in the home and society. Economically, intellectually and emotionally the home was the primary catalyst for meeting their needs.

We are obviously far from those days. Christian parents need not "the wisdom of the world" but "the foolishness of God" (see 1 Corinthians 1:20–25) in rearing their children—godly input from like-minded people who share our desire for children who will fulfill their destinies in God.

Discerning the difference between the two approaches is vital.

Role Confusion in the Home

Some time ago Sheree was at the grocery store with her entourage of blonde-haired "helpers"—only five of them at that point. The youngest were being pushed in one cart by Jesse while the older ones helped collect the food in a second cart—making their share of "suggestions" about purchases, of course!

When they got to the checkout counter, Sheree told me later, the children chatted with the friendly clerk. The last items to be scanned were some ingredients Sheree had selected to make chocolate chip cookies.

"Now this is amazing," the checker remarked to Sheree. "You have five children and you bake cookies, too? I didn't know people actually made homemade cookies anymore!"

Sheree told her she found real fulfillment being a homemaker. When asked how she could stand being at home all day with five children, Sheree replied that a relationship with Jesus Christ had given her a vision of motherhood and homemaking she'd never imagined possible.

The checker's final response was heartening. She told Sheree she enjoyed seeing such well-mannered children come into the store. (All those reminders about grocery store etiquette seem to have paid off!) She said she wished more young women valued motherhood as Sheree did.

As Sheree and the children trundled the cart out to the van, Sheree told me later, tears brimmed in her eyes. She couldn't have known how much Sheree had appreciated her words—and may not even have noticed that one of the purchases had been an in-home pregnancy test to confirm the conception of our sixth child!

Why are so many people, like that friendly grocery store checker, surprised at the fulfillment many stay-at-home moms find in their role? Is it because they view the "full-time homemaker" as a frumpy, uneducated woman who spends her day watching soap operas and scanning women's magazines?

And what about the current redefinition of manhood? Talk shows and magazines have been full of discussion about necessary changes in the way men act and view themselves. The media has joined in depicting (and ridiculing) men who typify one of two extremes—macho egotists who lack respect for women or weak-willed wimps who lack masculinity. Somewhere between these two extremes are men involved nationwide in the men's movement, meeting with support groups, going on retreats and trying desperately to find sensitivity *and* masculinity.

The biblical perspective of the role of both women and men in church, home and society is being increasingly questioned; and this is the fourth force at work in our society against the family. Wives who want to submit to their husbands and men who want to grow in leadership at home are "out of touch" with contemporary changes. Fewer boys, moreover, have a proper role model of the dad who provides for, leads, protects and cares for his family. Girls, likewise, have little or no exposure to someone who can train them to be wives, mothers and "keepers at home" (Titus 2:5, KJV).

Our children will find role models—on television, at the movies, at the desk next to them at school, at home. How will future generations be affected by the lack of value placed on biblical norms for roles in the home? Who will raise the children? Who will provide for their basic needs? Will traditional roles, as some have suggested, become a "historical curiosity" for our grandchildren?

Again, it is time for Christian parents to make some difficult choices for the sake of future generations. Years from now, when our children are grown, the new car and the deck furniture will be long forgotten. Not forgotten will be the memories etched in our children's hearts—memories of Dad praying for them when difficulties came; adjusting his schedule to be at their basketball games; taking them on family vacations; assuming leadership in the home; providing a biblical model of husband and father. Memories of Mom looking for creative ways to bless them with favorite meals and fun birthday parties; being there to comfort them when they were sick or injured or disappointed; giving the best of her time and energy to the family rather than to the job; finding joy in serving her family and relating to the Lord; offering an inspiring example of a woman who embraced and enjoyed her God-given privilege as a mother and homemaker.

In some cases, as with Sheree's sister who has been a single mom of two for many years, God has provided for their unique needs as a family, including the examples they will need for successful family life in the future. Others of us who are in a position to ensure that biblical roles don't become a historical curiosity have an exciting challenge ahead.

Worldliness

The October 27, 1986, issue of *U.S. News & World Report* pointed out that stress is no longer limited to the adult population, but is becoming increasingly evident in children. The article attributed some of the stresses children are facing to "a generation of status-conscious parents."

This perceptive conclusion by the secular world is aptly expressed by a bumper sticker I saw recently: *The man who dies with the most toys wins.* The price we parents are paying for our "toys"—VCRs, vacation homes, extra cars, computers, trendy clothes and other prizes to make life easier or more fun—may be much higher than what is displayed on the pricetag. I'm not suggesting that making purchases is always wrong. My own children enjoy working on the computer and watching wholesome movies on the VCR. The danger lies in sacrificing our children's need for our love, time and attention through material acquisition. The truth is, regardless of how many toys people have, they will face the God who made them in the same way they came into the world—with nothing.

Worldliness—and this is the fifth cultural barrage on the family—is to the Christian as cancer is to the body. It can slip in, subtle and undetected, until radical measures are needed to get rid of it. Simply stated, worldliness is the process of taking on the values, beliefs and priorities of a society that has rejected God.

You may be thinking, "Unbelievers *do* have wrong priorities, sinful habits and selfish values. I'm glad that I don't struggle with these things." Sheree and I felt this way until we began to see symptoms of worldliness in our own lives. Ask yourself questions like:

- Am I hesitant to obey God when it requires deviating from what my family, friends and neighbors think?
- Am I willing to sacrifice time and availability to the family to provide material pleasures?

- Does my sense of self-worth depend on where I live, what I drive, how I'm dressed or the job I hold?
- Do I make decisions for the family based on what others are doing, buying or thinking?
- Do I justify wrong decisions (i.e., purchases, children's friends, activities, entertainment) by minimizing their negative effect and saying, "Everyone else is doing it"?
- Am I willing to compromise godly standards of discipline and training of the children because "it's just too much work"?
- Am I hesitant to deprive the children of certain potentially negative relationships and activities because they may feel left out of their peer group or because we fear their rejection?

In considering some of the above, Sheree and I had to admit our temptation to say yes to some. These symptoms of worldliness are unlike those we grew up hearing about. Worldly individuals, to those of us who grew up in the Church, lied about spending the night with a friend to go to a wild party. They wore immodest clothing, smoked cigarettes behind the church building, were sexually active prior to marriage. Such definitions tend to "exempt" the rest of us from dealing with the less obvious but equally worldly manifestations. This issue became clear to Sheree and me several years ago concerning a situation with our oldest son.

Joshua had been asking for several years to play organized sports. As a father, I wanted to let him participate on a team but also wanted to consider his ability to withstand peer pressure. Nor did we want him exposed to the verbally harsh treatment many of my coaches had used to motivate me to play harder.

For weeks Sheree and I passed the posters announcing fall

sports sign-up. We discussed it thoroughly and decided that at age ten Joshua was ready. The next week Joshua spent the day with his closest friend, Andy. Because we have learned the value of other parents' input, Sheree asked Andy's mom for any thoughts she had when she picked Joshua up that evening. She informed her of an incident that happened with the boys that day. While playing in the swimming pool Joshua had reacted to a stressful situation by using bad language. We later confirmed he had heard it from one of the children in our neighborhood. This incident also confirmed our suspicion that Joshua was allowing this boy to influence him negatively.

We were left with two options. One was to dismiss the incident as a one-time occurrence typical of most boys Joshua's age. We would address it firmly and instruct him of the importance of monitoring the time he spent with his neighborhood friends. We could then see his involvement on the athletic team as an opportunity to practice resisting the pressure to conform to the example of his peers.

Advice we received from heartsick parents—those who had neglected to deal with similar warning signs of negative peer influence and now were dealing with wayward teens—caused us to choose a more radical option.

We saw this incident as a warning of Joshua's inability just yet to resist conformity to unbelieving friends. Without making him feel like a failure, we could strongly communicate our concern that he was not ready to be exposed regularly to potentially unwholesome influences and withdraw his registration from the team.

We chose to resist the easy way. We knew that in His mercy, God had given us a sign that just because participating in team sports is fun for the average ten-year-old didn't mean the timing was right for our son. We were unwilling to sacrifice the years we had invested in carefully training our son for a few months of fun.

When we told him he would not be playing on the team, Joshua cried and we comforted him. Yet he actually met our explanation with sincere appreciation. He worked through his disappointment and saw the wisdom of our decision. Our prayer for God to provide a better situation when he was mature enough to handle it came the following year when a man from our church became a Little League basketball coach. Joshua and Andy joined his team. It was a wonderful and memorable experience for our entire family.

Spiritual discernment and obedience to God can cost our children's apparent happiness. Yet worldliness seduces us to compromise godly standards for fleeting (or perilous!) pleasures. And loving parents are often willing to take dangerous risks to provide fun memories for our children.

At the risk of being accused of overprotectiveness, Christian parents must weigh the cost. Unchecked seeds of worldliness will grow like weeds in our children's lives. As I once heard, what parents do in moderation our children will do to excess.

You may be thinking: "I'm glad this worked for you, but I'm a single parent working to support my children. They're exposed regularly to other children at school and in the neighborhood. How can I possibly protect them from harmful peer influences?"

I empathize with your situation. In a day when an increasing number of women are forced into the workplace through divorce or financial necessity, the parental involvement that full-time motherhood provides is often impossible. The sense of frustration—and even guilt—can be overwhelming at times, especially when you begin to see some symptoms of negative peer influence in your children.

But even if you are unable to remove your children from a spiritually harmful environment, the solution to your challenges is like that of every concerned parent: Become more intimately involved in your children's lives. I hope the following brief suggestions will protect you from the "all-or-nothing" approach to parental awareness:

1. Expose your children regularly to positive influences (peers) and role models (other adults).

Just as those who do not share your Christian values can wrongly influence your children, those who share them can do so in a positive way. Over time, these relationships can create in your children a respectful desire to emulate their lifestyles.

2. Make personal sacrifices to become involved in your children's schools.

Set up regular conferences with their teachers. Offer to help with upcoming activities where parental involvement is solicited. Attend the parent-teacher meetings. This kind of initiative (which can be sacrificial at times) communicates to both your children and school officials that you desire to be aware of and involved with the people and activities that influence the majority of your children's time.

3. Familiarize yourself with your children's friends.

Have them over regularly for pizza or to join you on a family outing. Make your home the place where your children enjoy bringing their friends. Join in their games and activities and watch for potentially harmful relationships.

This approach to involvement in your children's lives may be costly. It may require using vacation time to attend a teacher conference or the school play. It may mean using a hard-earned Friday evening you've set aside to rest to entertain some very excitable ten-year-olds. But every hour sacrificed will pay dividends. You will be aware of those adults and children who may be influencing your child to compromise in certain areas. You will be better equipped to detect those individuals whose language, attitudes or activities are too much for your children to resist. And, most importantly, you will be communicating to all—including your children—that you desire to take seriously both the responsibility and the privilege of being deeply involved in their lives.

Economic Pressures

Our society has experienced some striking economic changes since our roots as a nation. Until the mid-1800s the family's income was based on the family business—Mom, Dad and the children working together on the farm or in a business that served the community. With the Industrial Revolution, Dad began leaving home to work in a factory or office while Mom stayed home to care for the children. In war times, mothers worked outside the home to provide for the family's needs.

After World War II the family seemed to return to "normal." The median age for first marriages fell for the first time in decades. The baby boom hit. Women gave up the jobs they had taken in record numbers during the war to stay home with their babies.

In the 1960s came a turnaround. Economic recession, a climbing divorce rate and a generation of me-seeking individualists contributed to a resurgence of the two-income and single-parent household.

In the 1990s, the children of these parents are becoming parents themselves—some with children fast approaching the teenage years. Many of us are apprehensive about how economic factors are affecting family life, particularly with the onset of another recession. Economic pressure, then, is the sixth societal force working against the family.

A special 1989 issue of *Newsweek* magazine entitled "What Happened to the Family?" suggested that "we have just begun to admit that exchanging old-fashioned family values for independence and self-expression may exact a price." The question is, What price will sheer economic need or our materialistic value system require of our children?

A divorced parent who must leave his or her young children to the care of others, or a mother who must work outside the home to make ends meet, must resist the guilt associated with loss of time with the children. The mother who must work outside the home because her husband is injured or is being educated to acquire better skills for the future can rest in knowing her circumstances are temporary. But every couple considering a two-income lifestyle for whatever reason must seriously weigh the benefits as over against long-term consequences.

We are privileged to know many couples who have wisely counted these costs. Some well-educated moms have elected to use their skills to generate income from home using the computer, sewing machine or telephone. Others have chosen to care for several extra children. Still other couples have learned to be content with a smaller home, an older car or the same worn furnishings for the advantages of full-time motherhood. And mothers we know who must work outside the home simply do their best, faithfully and unselfishly, to spend adequate time with their children.

Making money is a necessity. But sacrificing our children's emotional needs for the security of a strong bond with Mom and Dad is a risky price to pay.

*   *   *

Economic and other forces fighting against successful family living can sober us into evaluating what is truly important in life. Proverbs 22:3 says, "A prudent man foresees the difficulties ahead and prepares for them; the simpleton goes blindly on and suffers the consequences" (TLB). Our authority as Christians must be God's Word. Our values must reflect spiritual principles rather than worldly philosophies.

Let us examine ourselves in these critical areas, then, before we go blindly on and suffer the negative consequences of our decisions in the years ahead. God's grace will be abundant for any decisions we make in a faith response to Him.

4
Are Christian Families Exempt?

Benny

Ed and Carol married young and had four children in a few years. They became faithful members of their church. In fact, Ed became one of the leaders. As the children approached late elementary age, however, each became disinterested in church activities. They started complaining about getting up on Sunday morning and resented setting aside part of their allowance for the offering. Within a few years, Ed and Carol were waiting up late for staggering teenagers to arrive home from parties on Saturday night and paying outrageous insurance premiums due to several careless automobile accidents. Their family's church involvement was a thing of the past.

Stan and Julie did not raise their daughters in the church. When the girls were young teenagers, however, Stan and Julie were converted and got involved in a church with an active youth ministry. Like Ed, Stan became a respected church leader. One of the girls made a commitment to the Lord. The other attended meetings with no apparent desire to become a Christian. By the time the girls had graduated from high school, both had become involved with unbelieving young men. To this day, neither is walking with God.

Bob pastored a growing church in a small Southern town. His wife, Joan, ran a clothing store to supplement the family's income. Their two adolescent sons were active in the youth group. Behind the scenes, however, the boys were rebellious and spiritually apathetic. Their parents were fooled. Their friends were not. Within a few years they were using alcohol and experimenting with drugs.

Such stories are repeated in families across the nation. Many Christian parents assume that church membership and involvement in youth ministry will produce spiritually mature youngsters. Active churchgoing parents are stunned to learn that their "good" children are dabbling in substance abuse and premarital sex.

In his book on teenage sexuality, *Why Wait?*, author and speaker Josh McDowell says:

> A teenage relationship survey reveals that "religion-conscious girls are 86 percent more likely to say it's important to be a virgin at marriage than nonreligion-conscious girls. However, religion-conscious girls are only 14 percent more likely to be virgins than nonreligion-conscious girls."

Dr. Robert Laurent, author of *Keeping Your Teen in Touch with God*, confirms the point that many churchgoing young people remain unchanged by their religious experience:

> Over fifty percent of Christian teenagers will sit in church next Sunday morning. Within two years, seventy percent of them will have left the church, never to re-

> turn. . . . Gallup polls report that . . . sixty-five percent
> of evangelical teens never read their Bibles and thirty-
> three percent feel that religion is out-of-date and out-
> of-touch.

What a tragic response to Jesus' command that we be salt
and light in a world crying out for authentic New Testament
reality! This trend must be broken by a generation willing to
stand alone if necessary for the sake of the Gospel.

Having worked in youth ministry for several years before
pastoring the church I now serve, I have seen many of these
situations close-up. Like you, I want to do my part as a
parent to ensure that my own children truly grasp the Kingdom of God and avoid the kingdom of darkness.

But if being a Christian family does not ensure protection,
if parents who rear their children in church cannot be guar-
anteed positive results, then who can? What benefit is it to
take the children to all that the church offers if they have
little better chance to "turn out" than the unbelieving kids
down the street? And why do so many children, even
"preachers' kids," reject the Lord or become spiritually passive?

I don't have all the answers to such complex questions.
Sheree and I are not even sure of all the reasons why we,
who were both raised in churchgoing homes, went through
periods of worldly compromise. Yet we have seen the success of other parents whose children have escaped the snare
of teenage rebellion and emerged strong in spirit. We are
also seeing thrilling signs of spiritual passion in some of the
young men and women God has entrusted to us and other
parents we serve.

What, then, are some of the differences between young
people who refuse to bow to the seduction of the world and

those who succumb? Here are four suggested ways Sheree and I have found that Christian parents can miss the boat concerning their children's spiritual development.

Faulty Spiritual Foundation

Jesus never called people to attend Sabbath worship at some building, but to follow Him. The institutional Church today, on the other hand, speaks much of the involvement and little of discipleship. Parents whose personal relationship with the Lord is limited to church attendance will not inspire their children to follow after Jesus Christ, because Sunday morning Christianity alone does not equip us to handle the challenges of Monday morning parenting. Even young children can see through the unreality that only authentic discipleship can correct. This is the first way Christian parents can miss the boat.

As parents, we must provoke our children to godly jealousy by our devotion to the Lord. The way we resolve our marital conflicts, our attitude toward authority figures, our response to stressful situations, and the way we spend our time and money should all give testimony to our relationship with God. The most effective way to live a deepening Christian lifestyle that will inspire our children is in a church that emphasizes relationships over meetings.

Sheree's family was actively involved in such a church in their small town:

> Mom taught Sunday school. Dad served the pastor in various ways over the years. I sang in choirs, attended girls' camps and enjoyed summer Bible camps.
>
> As I approached my teenage years, I didn't escape many of the temptations of adolescence. By God's

grace, though, I was able to avoid becoming involved in much of what my friends were experiencing. Why? Not primarily because I was so involved in church activities. Like many of my friends, I could have left the Bible study to go to a party or sneak out with a boyfriend. Rather, I was concerned about disappointing my parents and those in the church, who had given so much of themselves to me over the years. Relationships, not meetings, were a safeguard for me.

Children won't be loyal to an institution; they are more likely to be loyal to people. Parents must be willing to invest the time to find a church that highlights the importance of relationships as taught in the book of Acts. The church we choose must be what one man has called an "organism, not an organization." Children will benefit from commitment to a church that is full of life, that teaches the Bible as the inspired, infallible Word of God; where successful family life is taught and modeled by the leaders; where relationships between families are encouraged and given opportunity to be fostered.

Joshua's experience with wanting to play organized sports is one of the many examples of this safety in relationships. If Andy's mom had not heard what she did or lacked the courage to pass the information on to Sheree, we may have made a serious mistake. Exposing our son prematurely to a peer group that did not support our value system would have threatened much that we had invested in him over the years.

Close, loving relationships provide a net of security for parents and children alike. Acquaintances based on brief Sunday morning interaction cannot offer the support, input, objectivity and encouragement that successful parenting requires.

Our sense of spiritual destiny, then, must go far beyond

attending meetings and church functions. We must be men and women captivated with a vision of usefulness to God. Young people respond to challenges, not rituals. An authentic Christian lifestyle is our most effective tool to create in our children a distaste for all this world can offer them. May it be said of us, as of Jesus, "Zeal for your house will consume me" (John 2:17).

Parents impassioned about their relationship with Jesus Christ will infect their children with zeal for God and His Church.

Misguided Priorities

The world clamors for our attention on every side. Mothers, as we have discussed, are pressed to resume outside employment to prove their worth (or self-worth). Fathers are driven toward career advancement to provide more "things" for the family—often becoming strangers to their wives and children in the process. Children are enticed by advertisers and friends who offer exciting products they think they can't possibly live without. The consequence of this pressured and materialistic lifestyle: lost time together as a family. This is the second way Christian parents can miss the boat.

Time is a precious resource, tragic if wasted, priceless if well-invested. Our children's futures, even their spiritual development, may be determined greatly by how we use the few years available to train them, to love them, and to build memories with them.

Some researchers suggest that lack of family time contributes significantly to the unhealthy state of the American family. Many families do not share regular evening meals together. *Newsweek* reported (August 18, 1989) that even the family vacation has suffered with a fourteen percent drop in length just since 1983. "Home has been left an impoverished place," reports *Time* magazine in its special fall 1990 issue on women, "little more than a dormitory, a spot for a shower and a change of clothes." In apparent response, a recent Gallup poll concluded that almost 75 percent of the nation feels that making financial sacrifices to give parents more time with their children is better than enjoying a higher standard of living (*Newsweek*, special issue, 1989).

I am not suggesting that more family time alone will cure the ills of America's families. Recent findings by social scientists Nick Stinnett and John DeFrain, on the other hand, cite adequate time spent together as one of the six characteristics found in healthy families.

Parents who maintain their priorities *will* invest the time needed for successful family life. This requires frequent evaluation. Ask yourself questions like:

- Am I spending time each day in meaningful interaction with my children?
- Am I attentive to and taking active interest in their lives (activities, hobbies, relationships)?
- Am I aware of their concerns, fears and anxieties?
- Do they feel free to come to me for advice or a listening ear?
- Do we have regular times together as a family (outings, family vacations, hobbies)?
- Am I diligent to put the distractions of the day aside when I am with the children? Do they feel they have my attention when we're together?
- Have I initiated some spontaneous time recently with the children (e.g., tossing the football, playing a board game, reading a favorite book, helping with schoolwork, taking a drive)?

If your answer to several of these questions is no, you may need to evaluate the amount of time you spend with your children. The sacrifices are not costly. It takes only minutes to turn off the television and offer to shoot a few baskets with your son or build a Lego castle with your young daughter. Little by little, such small investments of time add up to a reservoir of rich memories for your children.

One final caution in this area of priorities. As Christian parents, we must be careful that our church involvement does not communicate wrong messages to our children. Sheree and I try to maintain the priority of family life over church responsibilities, despite our full-time pastoral ministry. To protect our children from feeling that everyone else's needs require the best of Mom and Dad's time and energy, we guard our weekly "family day" together and our "date night" as a couple; we protect our weeks from becoming overbooked with church activities; we include the children in as many church activities as possible (even if their job is simply to greet people at the door or help prepare a meal for a new mother); and we look regularly for ways to spend spontaneous time with them while running errands or doing household chores.

Years of properly understood priorities will convince our children that activities like reading a newspaper, making and spending money, going to church meetings, watching television and doing yardwork are not nearly as important as developing our relationships as a family. The security this will bring will only add to their desire to emulate our lifestyle.

False Definition of Spirituality

I grew up hearing the phrase *That person is so heavenly minded he's no earthly good.* I never quite understood what that meant until I began to meet individuals who seemed to fit the description. "I'm not sure I can go out for dessert after the meeting," they would suggest. "I need to pray about it." Or someone would say he felt "led" to go to McDonald's rather than to the restaurant someone else had chosen, obligating everyone to drive further and be out later.

We must be careful as parents not to be heavenly minded in this way, or attempt to ascertain our children's spiritual health by mere externals—how frequently they bring up spiritual issues, how they seem to enjoy a particular gathering, how much they remember from the Sunday school lesson, or how expressively they worship God. These are important, yet overvaluing them can assure or concern us falsely and communicate a wrong concept of God to our children. This is the third way Christian parents can miss the boat.

The bulk of Jesus' teaching during His three-year ministry on earth is found in Matthew 5–7. He mentioned externals (prayer, fasting, giving) but emphasized character (humility, purity, spiritual hunger). At times He addressed the Pharisees' focus on outward evidences of spirituality by pointing up that the heart attitude behind these are more critical.

Like Jesus, and unlike the Pharisees, we must see our children's character development, especially in the early years, as a greater measure of their spiritual development than how often they read their Bibles, or how many verses they can quote.

This became an important issue to Sheree and me several years ago with Joshua. Sometime after his commitment to the Lord at age five, he started getting up early, as I have already mentioned, to read his Bible without any prompting from us. As a six- and seven-year-old, he participated enthusiastically in worship on Sunday mornings. We were very pleased with how our little man of God was developing.

A year later, however, we noticed he had stopped getting up to read in the mornings. On Sundays he was reserved during worship. Although he enjoyed the children's ministry, he wasn't as talkative on the way home about what he was learning. We began to wonder what was happening. Was he becoming bored with the church? Was this the beginning of a faltering relationship with the Lord? Was he in the beginning stages of spiritual apathy?

We soon realized we should not overreact. Some of what Josh was experiencing, we began to see, was developmental in nature, a spiritual "change of seasons." He was coming out of a season of childhood imitation of our relationship with the Lord into a needed season of developing his own walk. This realization enabled us to begin to help him work through this season instead of worrying fearfully that he was taking a wrong turn.

When Josh was about ten, I felt it was time to discuss it with him. I started by asking him questions about his relationship with the Lord. I got out the summary of his conversion Sheree had written the day after we prayed with Josh to make Jesus "boss" of his life. Then I decided to set aside some Saturday mornings to have breakfast with him to discuss a book for new believers that studied the foundations of our faith. At opportune times I began gently to discuss the self-consciousness that tempted him to be less expressive about his love for God and in sharing his faith with others.

The multi-year process of allowing Joshua to experience this change of seasons seemed long. We saw the need (as I mentioned earlier) to address various character weaknesses in him. Sometimes we reminded him that God wanted him to be unashamed of his Christianity. Our family worship times (inconsistent as they were!) encouraged all the children to be expressive in praising God and willing to pray aloud. And we prayed regularly for his increased hunger for God.

Something happened as Joshua approached twelve. His

interest was rekindled in the piano so he could be involved someday in leading worship. He asked for a new Bible with his name on the front because his old one was falling apart. He asked if he could serve by helping to duplicate tapes after the Sunday meetings. He accompanied several adults to pray for a friend of his who responded to a Sunday morning message. And his worship took on new expression.

Apparently our efforts over the years had begun to produce fruit. Sheree and I learned the important lesson of waiting patiently through a stage of spiritual development in one of our children without excusing any wrong attitudes. We were especially encouraged after a message Josh heard just recently in which young people were challenged to pursue a radical commitment to Jesus.

"What do you think of the message, Josh?" I inquired.

"I thought it was excellent," he responded enthusiastically. "I really learned a lot."

"Is there anything specific you think the Lord was saying to you?" Sheree asked.

"Well, the main thing I learned was that it's time for me to start being more serious about my relationship with the Lord. I'm not a little kid anymore, you know. And I need to get ready for whatever call He has on my life. It's time for me to grow up, Mom and Dad."

Oh, the joy of seeing your children respond to God! You and I can provide the proper environment for their spiritual growth, and we can pray our hearts out, but only God can draw them to Himself by His Spirit.

Recognizing the importance of our children's character development in the process is of vital importance. We must avoid the snare of evaluating their relationship with God simply on the basis of how they "perform" when they're with us. We will get into more specifics of this in later chapters.

Harmful Influences

The final way in which we as parents can miss the boat concerning relationships with the Lord is by allowing harmful influences in our children's lives. We can do our best to train them properly, only to see negative influences thwart many years of hard work.

Tom was reared in a Christian home. He was a responsive, happy child who was respectful toward adults and easy to get along with. When he was ten, his family moved to a new neighborhood. When a nearby family member became ill, Tom's mother took over a great deal of the nursing care and left his teenage sister looking after him after school.

Being in a new neighborhood was difficult and Tom, unfortunately, chose the wrong friends. Before long he was smoking cigarettes and shoplifting small items from a nearby store. By the age of fifteen Tom was on drugs and soon dropped out of high school. Unlike many of his friends who remain in bondage to sinful habits—some died drug-related deaths—Tom came to the end of himself in his mid-twenties and surrendered his life to Jesus Christ.

Although Tom took responsibility for his own wrong decisions, still the downward cycle began with the negative influence of one eleven-year-old boy who lived down the street. Tom's parents were Christians, but circumstances in the family and their own naïve confidence in their son's ability to withstand worldly pressures prevented them from seeing the handwriting on the wall.

Harmful influences don't always have such obviously negative results, but have you noticed how long it takes to rid your toddler's vocabulary of certain words he or she has heard only a few times in the neighborhood? Or what about the lasting impression a soap opera love scene can leave on the minds of our young children?

Protecting our children from dangerous influences requires what a friend of ours calls having a "gatekeeper's mentality." In Old Testament times gatekeepers were Levitical priests who protected areas of the Temple from uncleanness, theft or loss. This responsibility requires difficult decisions about limiting our children's exposure to certain neighborhood children. It means not involving our children in activities in which adults and children alike would not reinforce our standards. It's hard work, but it's well worth the effort. As the children mature in spirit, we extend their borders to situations in which they can be a positive influence on others rather than be influenced negatively by others. We'll be discussing this issue more in chapter 15.

Involving ourselves in a New Testament church, establishing and maintaining our priorities, emphasizing the importance of character development, and protecting our children from harmful influences will go a long way to protect them from leaving the church never to return again.

Are Christian families exempt from the heartache of wayward children who stray from God's purposes? Unfortunately, no. Yet by God's grace we can do our part to help our children experience the benefits of genuine Christian living. Nothing else we give our lives to will ever produce the joy that comes from seeing our children fulfill their destiny in Him.

5
Shaping Their Concept of God

Sheree

Have you ever noticed how much your values, attitudes, behavior and habits were influenced by your parents? Maybe you embraced their example in these areas. Or perhaps you reacted negatively to them and purposely developed just the opposite. In either case, your upbringing—and especially your parents' example—was probably a significant factor in who you are today.

Consider the ways you are like your parents. Maybe you find yourself preparing certain foods you enjoyed while growing up. The neatness standards in your home today may mirror those that were modeled for you. Perhaps you catch yourself parroting your parents' phrases when relating to your children. As a youngster, you may even have promised yourself you would *never* be like your parents in various ways. Yet, even so, you have not escaped the influence they had during your formative childhood years. Your attitude toward work, political leaders, church involvement, financial debt or family vacations was at least partially influenced by your parents.

We are likewise influencing our children. What an awesome responsibility we have as parents! The values and attitudes with which we raise our little ones have the potential to influence generations to come, as our children duplicate us, and their children follow in turn.

Benny and I have already seen this principle in practice in little ways with our children. My visible dislike for anything in the house that crawls or flies has already had its effect on our daughters, Jaime and Janelle; they scream for one of the boys whenever they see a bug. Several of the children have benefited from my enjoyment of homemade crafts and now sell their own handiwork to earn income. And their love for having people in our home ("Oh, good! Is somebody coming over for another meeting where you eat cookies?") has, I hope, been modeled by a mom who enjoys extending hospitality.

Benny's influence is equally evident in the children. Most obvious is their gleeful response to an offer of anything chocolate. Even the girls love football. The boys are eager to wear dress shirts and ties many Sundays because they want to be like Daddy, who wears a suit to the office most mornings. Their willingness to do their best to keep their rooms neat is mainly due to wondering when Dad will show up unexpectedly to see what's lurking under their beds.

These simple examples help us see how we subtly influence our children. Other interactions are much more critical for their future, particularly those that shape their concept of God.

Adults who find it difficult to enjoy the unconditional acceptance and unmerited grace of God wrongly assume their relationship with Him is based upon how well they perform. They struggle frequently with inadequacy as Christians, thinking they never "do enough" or pray enough or give enough to merit God's favor.

Those who slide to the other extreme may breeze through life wondering why others feel guilty so often. When they find it difficult to overcome sinful habits, they remind themselves that, after all, "Christians aren't perfect, just forgiven." They realize that spiritual disciplines are important for spiritual growth and intend to make regular time with God a priority . . . next year.

What causes us to tend to fall into one of these categories? Personality is certainly a factor. Individuals with perfectionistic tendencies, for example, would have a more legalistic and performance-oriented approach to God. Those whose personalities are more "easygoing" would probably be more lax about discipline.

Personality traits provide part of the shaping process in our concept of God, but an equal, if not greater, factor is the influence of others. In specific terms, our concept of God seems to be influenced most by our relationship with our parents and other significant adults during childhood.

I was raised in a loving family with three siblings. My parents had their share of difficulties over the years. Finances were usually tight, but with a few short-term exceptions Mom stayed at home to care for us. Mom and Dad faced struggles in their relationship over the years but always worked things out.

Affection was a big part of our family life. Both of my parents felt comfortable giving and receiving hugs and kisses and we all often exchanged "I love you's." They made many personal sacrifices to provide piano lessons, new dresses for school dances and occasional trips to McDonald's. I was always secure in their love and acceptance even though they had fairly strict codes of conduct.

Our family faced many difficulties during my childhood: Mom's brother was burned to death in a house fire; several family members struggled with alcoholism; Dad suffered for years with coronary problems; other family members lost small children in tragic ways; and my older brother was paralyzed by a swimming accident at age 21. Yet through the hardships, Mom and Dad helped us to weather the storms together. Their faith and perseverance were the stabilizing factors the rest of us depended on.

I see now how much my relationship with the Lord has its roots in my upbringing. I have never expected the Christian life to be without difficulties, and I don't generally respond to problems with a "Why me, Lord?" mentality. I can believe that God is my loving Father—warm and compassionate—because of the wonderful relationship I shared with my dad until his death in 1976. My parents' commitment to punishment for violating their standards of behavior taught me that sin always has consequences. And the frequency with which we laughed and played together helps me approach my relationship with the Lord with expressive enthusiasm.

Benny's childhood years were less disciplined and affectionate, but his parents' sacrifices and commitment still led him to a deep relationship with his heavenly Father:

> I grew up the youngest of three boys. Since finances were tight for us, Daddy officiated for various team sports to earn income in addition to his full-time job. Mother held part-time jobs on and off over the years and began to work full-time when I was in elementary school. Even with the demands on her time and three sons who took advantage of her willingness to serve, Mother was a well-organized homemaker. Our home was always neat, the laundry kept up and we enjoyed bacon and eggs for breakfast before school. I have come to deeply appreciate this important expression of her love for us.

Daddy's father was murdered when Daddy was only two years old so fatherhood had never been modeled for him. My parents married when Mother was barely fifteen and Daddy was 21. The financial and emotional tasks of raising the children, who began to come quickly, were understandably difficult.

Their schedules did not allow much time for spontaneous interaction with us. This was compounded by a family tragedy. After three boys, my parents were delighted to have a daughter when I was six years old. Shortly after her sixth birthday, however, she died of acute leukemia. The years of fear, uncertainty, dashed hopes for her recovery, and stress that preceded her death took a toll on all of us. Our family life suffered. There was little emphasis on growing together as a family.

Although expressions of love were infrequent, I knew my parents loved me. I understood that their commitment to working hard over the years to provide for us was evidence of their affection.

My earliest memories are of staying with relatives in Alabama. We were a churchgoing family, but during their teenage years my older brothers lost interest in the church and seemed constantly to get into trouble. I remember frequent arguments between them and my parents or between themselves over who would use the car, how late they would stay out or why borrowed money had not been repaid. My parents tried unsuccessfully to curb their behavior and sometimes chose to keep peace in the home by ignoring it.

I was, in turn, gaining a reputation as "Charlie and Andy's little brother." Over the years I learned that, like them, I could get a lot of attention by making wrong choices. By age fifteen I had been to court several times for grand larceny and breaking and entering. I was given a three-year suspended sentence at a boys' penitentiary and was still on probation at my conversion at age sixteen when my life changed dramatically.

I can still be somewhat introverted. Expressing emotion has never come easily for me (unless I'm watching a Washington Redskins football game!). Being raised in a home with few visible expressions of love added to the awkwardness I can feel in relating to the Lord with emotion. Though I frequently feel stirred during worship, I find it challenging to express myself with the emotional ease others find natural.

Because my parents were frequently unaware of my activities, I suffered the consequences of my decisions only when the police became involved. This has contributed to my self-deception at times toward personal sin and its consequences: I simply got away with too much as a boy. Like Sheree's, my upbringing showed me that struggles are part of life—even the life of a Christian—and taught me the options with which I can respond to them.

Our point in sharing these thoughts is to show the influence a home environment plays in fashioning a child's ability to respond to God.

In other words, thinking that our children will have an accurate perception of God simply because they are well-churched is naïve. We must embrace actively the responsibility to help them become spiritually mature. In fact, as parents our primary goal must be to pursue passionately whatever will ensure that our children fulfill their destinies in God. Like Paul, we desire to see our children "take hold of that for which Christ Jesus took hold of [them]" (Philippians 3:12).

Webster defines *maturity* as "a state of full development; maximum potential; being full grown or ripe; complete and ready." Children whose role models offer distorted or negative perceptions of God will not become ripe for usefulness to Him. They may doubt His love and acceptance, view Him as frustrated or irritated by their failures or wonder if they are performing well enough to warrant His favor. Such misconceptions will hinder them from having the confidence to embrace God's call on their lives.

Creating the right kind of home environment begins when we parents assess our children's true needs. Parents today are tempted to let their children determine their own "needs"—usually things they want to gain acceptance from their peers. Many parents, consequently, focus inordinately on providing material things at the expense of the legitimate needs of our children.

What are our children's basic needs? Here are seven crucial ones.

Parents' Availability

We can help our children feel our unconditional love and availability, the first basic need, in two essential ways, both related to spending time with them.

One, we must make room in our schedules for specific activities with our children. As with monetary investments, we need to resist the myth of "quality versus quantity" time. Imagine approaching your banker with, "Sir, I know I'm only depositing one dollar in your bank, but it's a special silver dollar that my father gave me years ago. There's not a scratch on it! Surely this warrants my receiving more interest than normal!"

Likewise, assuming that the quality of limited time we spend with our children is more important is equally foolish. Yes, it takes time to fill up the little swimming pool in the backyard on a hot summer day. It takes time to play your toddler's favorite board game with him. It takes time to attend the basketball games and piano recitals and Christmas plays. But over the years each small investment grows into a return you will value above all others.

Two, we must avoid giving them what I call "busy signals." Often unintentionally we can communicate hurtful messages to our children—messages that suggest we are unavailable to them.

Several months ago I was busy preparing dinner when five-year-old Joey came in.

"Hi, Mom!" he said in his usual enthusiastic way. "What ya doing?"

"I'm fixing dinner, honey."

"What are we having?"

Frustrated because his questions made me lose track of the number of teaspoons of baking soda I had put into a bowl of flour, I said, "Honey, why don't you go outside and play with Jesse?"

My irritation was apparent in my tone of voice. "I'm sorry, Mommy," he said as he headed toward the door.

Ugh! This thirty-second exchange could never be retracted. It was over and our son felt as though he had done something wrong by being curious about his mom's activities. If repeated time after time, year after year, whom would Joey go to with teenage concerns about girls or schoolwork? Probably not Mom.

In the midst of adult concerns and responsibilities it can be difficult to "unplug" and give our children the spontaneous ear they need, but we must if we are to help them form a correct concept of God. The Bible is full of references to "the riches of his kindness, tolerance and patience," which ultimately lead us "toward repentance" (Romans 2:4). The example we set will help them believe that "as a father has compassion on his children, so the Lord has compassion on those who fear him" (Psalm 103:13). The foundation of their friendship with God can best be laid by parents committed to creating an environment of love, kindness and patience in the home.

Proper Role Modeling

We have already discussed how much our actions, attitudes and responses influence our children, in both positive and negative ways.

We may take great pains to see that they are instructed in godliness, but instruction alone will never train children effectively. They learn more by watching our behavior. Thus, their second basic need for shaping a right concept of God is proper role models.

Some years ago I decided to teach our older children character qualities by having them study the fruit of the Spirit listed in Galatians 5:22. We talked about each quality, drew pictures and thought of appropriate songs. I felt good about doing something "systematically" spiritual with our children. Unfortunately, when then-five-year-old Jaime ended up in tears of frustration over her attempts to draw a picture of "peace" (who could blame her?), we set the idea aside (just as I had many other good systematic ideas over the years!).

Maximum training is achieved when children are taught by both words and actions. They may not remember talking about love, joy and patience, but they will remember the ways—both positive and negative—that we demonstrate these qualities for them.

In 2 Thessalonians 3:9 Paul says, "We . . . make ourselves

a model for you to follow." We parents will grow in confidence to offer ourselves as models for our children as we identify and try to overcome our own weaknesses. For Benny and me, the process has been difficult and the changes painfully slow. We know we cannot become "perfect examples" for our children. (Anytime we might be tempted to think otherwise, something always happens to bring us back to reality!) But we can try to take seriously our need to recognize and change areas of harshness, impatience, selfishness or greed—to please God, certainly, but also to become models worth emulating.

Encouragement

The author of Hebrews exhorts us to "encourage one another daily . . . so that none of you may be hardened by sin's deceitfulness" (3:13). Encouragement is our children's third basic need, an integral part of their relationship with their parents.

The word *encourage* means "to put courage into." Our children, as young men and women, will need a lot of courage to withstand today's pressures. A parental offering of affirmation, appreciation and rewards in their early years will go a long way toward providing a strong foundation for their critical teenage years.

Our son Jesse, now seven years old, has always been big for his age. In fact, the doctor who delivered him suggested that if babies were like puppies, his hands and feet were sure indicators that he would be a big man! Since his size has hindered his coordination somewhat, he has been slightly less proficient in certain skills, especially sports.

Over the years we have sometimes seen his frustration over not doing as well at tossing a football, running or swinging a bat as his peers. It was especially difficult when his younger brother of nearly two years, Joey, began to outrun him and score more touchdowns. We continued to encourage Jesse, letting him know how much we appreciated his attempts to maintain a good attitude when he lost a race or struck out at bat. Yet at times our hearts were broken, wondering if he noticed he was often the last one chosen for a game and hoping his self-worth would be preserved.

Some time ago just before dinner, we were interrupted by a very excited young boy. "Mommy! Daddy! You won't believe it! I scored my first touchdown!" We both joined him in clapping and dancing around the dining room.

This was a significant moment for him. Not just because he had finally achieved something he had worked so hard for, but because he had persevered through the many disappointments along the way. We were delighted to share his joy, and were grateful that our encouragement and that of his siblings over the years had helped him reach this moment.

Encouragement may not always come naturally. Here are some suggestions to help you.

1. Encourage character over accomplishment.

Jesse's victory wasn't primarily athletic. It was a victory over discouragement, pouting, wanting to give up and feeling inferior. Saying, "Honey, thank you for being so patient" communicates more than, "I knew you could make a touchdown!" Emphasizing children's character also protects them from becoming performance-oriented.

2. Affirm for legitimate reasons.

Thanking our children for working hard is effective because it is not necessarily communicating they did a completely acceptable job. It would be wrong, for instance, to allow them to think that doing everything to clean the bedroom but making the bed is O.K. Hence, "Thank you for working so hard to clean your room" can be lovingly followed by, "Now all you need to do is make your bed."

3. Acknowledge specific qualities.

Many parents fail to see the importance of being specific with encouragement. We can assume that "Hey, you're special" is adequate. Children benefit most from hearing specific encouragement for their neatness, kindness toward their siblings, cheerfulness, politeness, etc.

4. Watch your countenance and voice tones.

Attempting to encourage your children while watching television or reading a book will probably be ineffective. Maintain eye contact, smile and let your child feel your appreciation or affirmation.

The key to encouraging our children consistently is sensitivity toward their needs. We should *look* for things to encourage in them, remembering how much encouragement blesses and motivates us adults. Proverbs 11:27 says that "he who seeks good finds good will." Finding good and then acknowledging it goes a long way to cause our children to desire a relationship with the God of all encouragement.

Discipline

The fourth of our children's basic needs is for clear boundaries and loving, consistent discipline. This subject could fill a book, and has, many. We will discuss discipline in a later chapter but mention it here to underscore it as one of our children's needs, rather than simply a tactic for dealing with bad behavior.

Pediatrician and author Dr. T. Berry Brazelton is often interviewed and quoted in the media. He feels that clear

behavioral boundaries are important for our children because they feel reassured by having limits set. "It is the only
way they learn," he says. A generation of parents who grew
up with childrearing philosophies that deemphasized the importance of clear boundaries and consistent discipline needs
desperately to hear this message.

Parental unwillingness to meet a child's need for discipline, including applying the rod of correction, is often
rooted either in selfishness or ignorance. We must overcome
any misconceptions we have about child discipline for the
sake of our children. Effective discipline is both loving and
firm—and is always born out of a heart of unconditional
acceptance for the child.

As a plaque in a friend's house reads: "It is better to build
children than to repair men." We must be committed to
consistent and loving discipline to prepare our children for
the discipline of God and protect them from the reproofs of
life.

Respect for Authority

A fifth basic need our children have is to appreciate and
respect authority. We will be covering this critical subject
in the next chapter. It is important to note at this point
that respect for authority is not something we can simply
hope for for our children. Neither is it selfish to want our
children to refrain from arguing with and resisting us.
Rather, our children need to develop respectful attitudes
toward those in authority to succeed in this life. And it begins in the home.

Trust

Our children must be able to trust their parents completely, their sixth basic need. Any successful relationship is

built on a foundation of trust. Married couples must be able to trust one another's love and fidelity. Employers must trust their employees' honesty and abilities. Likewise, children need to have confidence that their parents' words and lifestyles can be trusted.

Today's children are under a lot of pressure. They face some stresses that previous generations never thought of— nuclear war, sexual molestation, their parents' divorce, being abducted, AIDS. Their fears are compounded by uncertainty about adults. When they hear of various traditionally trustworthy people like political and religious leaders bowing to greed and immorality, young people are confused and disillusioned. "Whom can I trust?" they ask.

Jane was a non-Christian teenage girl who frequented the youth meetings we led some years ago. She was excessively shy but seemed willing to talk with me after the gathering one Saturday night.

I offered to take Jane out for ice cream to discuss her relationship with the Lord. We talked for several hours. Jane was open to Christianity, and as I listened to her questions I soon realized that some of her hesitance to commit her life to the Lord lay in a faulty image of God's character. Then Jane revealed that she had been sexually molested as a child by her father.

"How can I trust that what you're saying about God is true, Sheree? And how can I believe that God loves me unconditionally? My father said he loved me, and that that was why he did the things he did!" Her inability to trust others— especially God—was rooted in the perverted example of trust she grew up with.

It's time for parents to exhibit the integrity worthy of our children's trust. This includes our motives, our protection and provision, our love, and our word.

Trust is often eroded in the early years by seemingly insignificant things—unkept promises, repeated threats of disciplinary action that never came about, forgotten commitments. Over the years, such incidences jeopardize our children's confidence that Mom and Dad can be trusted and leave one of their basic needs unmet.

Stable Home Life

The seventh and final need is our children's deep yearning for a stable home environment. A home life with two parents who love them and each other is the best safeguard against the pressures today's children face. Yet we shouldn't presume that simply sharing a home with our children ensures their emotional stability. Providing a secure environment means more than sleeping, eating and watching television in the same house.

As parents, the best thing we can do for our children is first to cultivate our relationship with the Lord, and next continue to deepen our relationship with our spouse. Many a child's greatest fear is that their parents will someday divorce. They need to feel confident in the fact that Mom and Dad will invest whatever work is necessary into making their relationship successful. Viewing that relationship as permanent affects their eventual trust in God's covenantal love.

What about those who, through divorce or unwed pregnancy, are single parents? Single parents can still provide a warm and caring home atmosphere. And they will benefit from close connections with their churches.

Some churches organize support groups or special meetings for single parents. Others encourage families to reach out to single parents and their children, including them in family outings or vacations. Still others encourage fathers in the church to reach out to the children of single mothers to offer a man's influence or simply to provide—especially for the boys—a man to go camping or do some batting practice with. Any initiative could help offset the anxiety and isolation many single parents can feel, especially in churches with an emphasis on family ministry.

To Christian parents, nothing should take precedence over our desire to see our children come into an intimate relationship with Jesus Christ. We have, to a large degree, the ability to shape their concept of God. The task seems overwhelming at times, especially when we catch a glimpse of how easily they view God in relation to us ("Mommy, does Jesus have blond hair and crooked teeth like Daddy?"). The assignment doesn't come without the necessary resources to complete it. The rest is in His hands.

6
Respect: A Crucial Foundation

Sheree

One of the most challenging experiences for parents is passing this test of sanity: the candy display at the grocery store checkout. I have often wondered why store managers deliberately add to their employees' stress levels by forcing them to listen to screaming toddlers who manipulate their parents into quieting them with a bag of M&Ms.

At a recent trip to the store, a young mother with one child was ahead of me in line.

"Mommy, I want some candy," the boy said. He looked to be about four years old.

"No, honey. It's too close to dinner," his mother replied.

"But I want some, I'm hungry," he whined as he strained toward the candy counter.

"I said no. We'll eat when we get home. Now don't ask me again."

"I want some candy!" he wailed, yanking on her arm. He began to cry, pleading that he couldn't wait.

"Oh, all right. Now shut up," she snapped, handing him a candy bar. Amazingly, his crying stopped immediately and he chattered pleasantly about his day with some friends at the playground. As we left the store that afternoon I couldn't help but be concerned for the kind of problems this mother may have to face when her son becomes a teenager.

Now why would I think that? you may ask. Don't most young children react similarly when they don't get their way? How could crying over a candy bar at age four lead to problems in adolescence?

As we have mentioned, developing a child's character in the early years is critical to his or her attitudes in the future. A toddler gets away with showing disrespect toward his mother's decision about a candy bar. Her request for him not to bring up the subject again falls on deaf ears. Year after year she makes similar demands with no consequences when they are ignored. The boy learns that if he protests enough and can embarrass or unnerve Mom, he eventually gets his own way. At ten he may manipulate her into purchasing an expensive new bike, the kind his friends have. At thirteen he may ignore her protests and attend a party at the house of a friend whose parents are out of town. By sixteen their home may be strife-ridden with his resistance to her curfews and objections to the company he keeps or the activities in which he is involved.

Over the years we have been aware of many heartbreaking situations that have developed in just this way. Seeds of disrespect left unchecked will only grow. They cannot help but affect a child's spiritual condition.

The Importance of the Fear of the Lord

Why is it important to require our children to show us respect? The answer is clear. Children who respect their parents become adults who honor God. The type of respect that is due their heavenly Father is referred to in Scripture as the "fear of the Lord."

There are five uses for the word *fear* in the Bible. Four refer to fear as we commonly think of it—being afraid or startled. Yet, when alluding to the Lord, the word for *fear* really means godly reverence or awe.

This is the kind of fear that shows honor and devotion. The protection children need from worldly seduction is grounded in an attitude of reverence for God and His standards of conduct.

The Bible is full of references to the fear of God. Let's look at twelve characteristics from the book of Proverbs that will help us see the importance of building this foundation in our children's lives.

1. The fear of God is the beginning of knowledge (1:7). The foolish have no fear of God. Proverbs 22:15 states that foolishness is bound in a child's heart and must be removed in order for godly knowledge to be formed.

2. The fear of God promises a response from Him on our behalf (1:28–29).

3. The fear of God is a choice (1:29). Our children can choose to reverence God and His standards and experience the blessings of their obedience. Or they can reject them and suffer the consequences. Similarly, they can be trained to respect or reject our standards.

4. The fear of God leads to blessings: discernment (2:1–5); protection (2:11); peace (3:1–2); long life (4:10); health (4:20–22); and honor (22:4).

5. The fear of God causes hatred of evil (8:13). Hating evil will cause our children to flee from it and experience the fruit of holy living.

6. The fear of God leads to wisdom (9:10). Our children will need wisdom to make right choices for their careers, marriage partners, friends, activities.

7. The fear of God prolongs life (10:27).

8. The fear of God creates strong confidence (14:26, KJV). Confident, courageous young people are better able to resist peer dependency by being able to stand alone when necessary.

9. The fear of God is a fountain of life (14:27; 19:23).

10. The fear of God promises instruction in important life decisions (15:33, KJV).

11. The fear of God rewards us with wealth, honor and life (22:4). Individuals who honor God and His Word are positioned for spiritual riches and abundant life.

12. The fear of God protects us from envy (23:17). So many children are entrapped by wishful comparisons rooted in insecurity, discontent and low self-worth.

Glance over this list again briefly. What parent would not want his or her children to experience the incredible blessings listed above? Yet so many don't realize the importance of preparing our children to revere God by training them to respect and honor us.

Children Are Not Born Respectful

Our experience as parents has convinced Benny and me—as most parents have found—that children must be trained to show respect to those in authority in their lives. Aren't most three-year-olds tempted to cry or whine when told they can't have another cookie? Wouldn't most seven-year-olds get that "Oh, Mom, do I *have* to?" look on their faces when asked to empty the garbage? Haven't teenagers been known to argue about things they know very little about?

And could it be that leaving such issues unaddressed in our children would lead to an eighteen-year-old who responds to God's direction for his future with "Lord, do I *have* to?" A twenty-year-old who reacts against God for "limiting" his choice of a wife to godly Christian young women? A young adult who contends pridefully with God over important decisions about her goals and plans?

The popular belief that children are born basically good and need help only to "allow their little personalities to develop" is in opposition to God's Word. David spoke of the sin nature and a bent toward wickedness being present even before birth (Psalm 51:5; 58:3). This doesn't mean, of course, that we should demean our children. Rather, it equips us lovingly and consistently to train them away from sin and toward godly living. Teaching our children to honor and respect us requires clear standards, loving restraints and consistent discipline.

I was discussing this issue of respect recently with a close friend, a mother of two young children. She told me how her four-year-old often responded with whining or angry outbursts when he was not allowed to get his own way. He sometimes yelled "No!" when asked to pick up his toys, argued when he couldn't have a snack before lunch or flopped around angrily in the chair he had been asked to sit in for a quiet time of looking at books. I was inspired by her discernment that this was an issue of respect. She was determined not to be complacent about such behavior and disciplined him appropriately, realizing that allowing such things to continue would only convince him that he was in control of the rules and standards in the home, not Mom and

Dad. She was unwilling to settle for such behavior as "normal toddler development" and then have to deal with more serious manifestations of dishonor in later years.

Now, let's turn our thoughts to four essential ingredients of raising respectful children: authority, honor, standards and parental confidence.

Respect Involves Authority

Children cannot respect parents who don't command respect. Many children lack respect for their parents who, like the woman in the grocery store, do not rightly use their God-given position of authority in the home.

Well-exercised parental authority helps our children understand the government (that is, rule and reign) of God. God's place of rulership in their lives is first displayed in the parent-child relationship. Colossians 3:20 exhorts children to "obey [their] parents in everything, for this pleases the Lord." Children who are required to respond to this important command will ultimately be positioned to receive the gift of God's Spirit, given to those who obey Him (Acts 5:32).

Parental authority is an awesome responsibility. Many parents, fearful of making mistakes and being blamed by their children in later years for being "too strict," cower from offering the leadership their children inwardly crave. Children benefit from knowing Mom and Dad are "in charge."

Parents—not young children—should choose their bedtimes, television shows, meal menus, playmates and time spent on hobbies and homework. Parents must monitor what kind of music their children listen to and the books and magazines they read. We must set and enforce the standards of neatness in their rooms. And we must be willing to enforce whatever disciplinary action is necessary when they resist our authority. As our children approach adolescence, we can begin to consider their ideas and suggestions on these issues.

Our Jesse was particularly expressive when he was younger about any limitations we placed on him. Just after he turned two he would sometimes throw temper tantrums when told he was being left with a babysitter or that he couldn't have any more juice until he finished his dinner. For several months we dealt with kicking, screaming, hitting and long crying sessions in which he threw himself on the floor. We never knew what might set him off.

With many prayers and tears we sought God for a way to help Jesse learn that he was not in control in our home. We wanted to demonstrate our authority in his life, knowing that this would bring him security and peace. As with most challenging children, the very thing he was reacting to—restraints and boundaries—was what he inwardly desired from us.

We researched what various "experts" suggested about dealing with temper tantrums in young children. Our options, we were told, were to throw water onto his face, walk away and ignore him, lock him in his room until he gained control of himself, reason with him quietly to calm down or go ahead and give in to what he wanted because he would forget about it the next day anyway. After all, one psychologist said, he was probably just exerting a normal amount of independence for his age and would outgrow this behavior in a few years.

A few years? What about the adults we know who, although they don't fall on the floor kicking and screaming, have immature reactions or an equal lack of inner control over their emotions? Why didn't they grow out of their angry and selfish responses? Besides, could we deprive our son of the restraints that he seemed to be asking for? Ignoring it felt to us like ignoring an adult who attempts suicide—a desperate cry for help with inner turmoil and fear.

We are delighted to testify of God's faithfulness in Jesse's life. Through consistent, firm and loving correction of his behavior we were happy to see the tantrums gradually disappear. As an eight-year-old he experiences the mild emotional responses typical of his age and maturity, but he is cooperative and respectful toward us and other adults. Since that season of tantrums we have been pleased to meet other parents who took a stand for loving authority and experienced similar results.

Respect Involves Honor

Exodus 20 lists the Ten Commandments God gave to Moses. Of all the important issues to choose from for this most crucial listing, God included honoring parents among them (verse 12). This is the only Commandment given with a promise: "Honor your father and your mother, so that you may live long in the land the Lord your God is giving you." Our motives as parents should be to ensure their receiving the blessings that come from obeying God's command.

Benny and I have met many parents who have every desire to teach and train their children. They long to see their children grow in devotion to God. They are willing to invest the time into training their children to be polite, responsible and considerate of others. Yet they find their attempts are not producing the fruit they desire. Upon investigation, the frequent reason is that there is a disrespectful attitude in the children toward one or both parents. A child who does not honor his or her parents will not accept their teaching and cannot be trained properly.

Several years ago we met Jim and Susan when they were invited by a member of our church to a parenting seminar we were conducting. Jim was especially interested in what the Bible says about childrearing. In fact, he was desperate for answers. He and Susan, unbelievers, had invested many hundreds of dollars for their not-yet-school-aged daughter, Debbie, to be evaluated and treated by child psychiatrists. They were unnerved that her anger, excessive moodiness, lack of response to affection and overall misery had earned for her the labels *hyperactive* and *schizophrenic*.

The first answer to their cry for help came quickly when Jim committed his life to Jesus Christ. He and Susan began attending church and within months, she, too, became a Christian. They sought Christian counsel about their relationship with Debbie and realized that they had made several mistakes, as all parents do. They began to relate to her with greater acceptance, warmth and affection, and gave consistent discipline. They agreed that while they needed to make changes in their relationship to her, she also needed to learn to honor them.

They also realized that Debbie showed greater disrespect toward Susan than Jim. Jim committed himself to supporting his wife totally in the discipline and training of the child by giving Susan encouragement and honor in their daughter's presence. This was an important step. A child will not honor his mother if his father doesn't, and he will not honor his father if his mother doesn't. Susan, in turn, sought to overcome harshness and idle threats with Debbie. She and Jim both agreed to deal consistently with Debbie's hostile and disrespectful attitude toward them.

Miracles didn't happen overnight. Yet little by little Jim and Susan began to notice signs of change in their daughter. Her attitudes became less offensive and reactionary. She seemed less withdrawn emotionally. As they enforced their standards, it became easier to instruct her in other areas. One wonderfully unexpected result came a few months later when Debbie, for the first time in her life, told her daddy she loved him!

More and more Debbie proved that the physicians who labeled her were wrong. Challenges still arise for Jim and Susan, but in a few short years, they were well on the way to recovery as a family.

Respect Involves Standards

Some time ago our then three-year-old Janelle, whose nickname is Missy, came in from playing outside with her siblings to talk with me.

"Mommy, will you come outside with me?" she asked.

"I'm sorry, honey. I can't play with you right now because I'm folding laundry," I responded.

"Mommy, you're funny," she said with a grin. "I don't want you to play. I want you to put a line on the sidewalk to show me where my boundary is."

"Missy, you know where the boundary is. It's right by the neighbor's mailbox."

"I know, Mommy. But I want you to make a mark on the sidewalk so I'll know when I'm disobeying."

I was just about to commend her for wanting so much to please Mommy and Daddy when she interrupted my thoughts with, "Because I might decide to disobey!"

Oh, well! The daughter I thought wanted to please us really wanted to get that strange charge that comes from deliberately doing the opposite. Like walking on the grass when the sign forbids you to do so.

Janelle knew the general vicinity of her outdoor boundaries, but in order to show blatant disrespect she needed specifics. It wouldn't be as much fun to wander past the neighbor's mailbox as it would to step purposely over my chalk mark on the sidewalk. (She decided not to, by the way!)

Setting the standard for conduct is always the responsibility of the one in authority rather than the one under authority. Does your boss allow you to determine when you arrive at the office each day? Does your local police force consult you before posting speed limits? Why is it that we understand the importance of authority in our lives and yet hesitate to exercise it in the lives of our children?

Setting standards, of course, always implies penalties for breaking them (see Romans 4:15 and 5:13). In determining our standards for the way our children respond to us, we must also establish a reasonable penalty for disobedience. Not enforcing our rules may even produce greater disrespect than not having rules in the first place.

Benny and I have developed five basic criteria for respectful responses from our children. You may find them helpful in considering this issue in your family.

First, we require our children to use a respectful tone of voice. When we call them they may answer with "Yes, sir?" or "Yes, Mommy?" rather than "What?" or "Huh?" When we ask them to serve in some way ("Jaime, would you straighten the living room, please?"), they may say, "Sure, I'd be glad to" or, "O.K., Mom." "Can't Joshua do it this time?" or "I wanted to go outside!" are not permissible responses.

Second, we require obedience before discussion. Especially in the early years, children must learn the importance of immediate obedience. They are not owed an explanation for everything, partially because their reasoning abilities are not mature enough to handle the explanation anyway. Arguing is not acceptable at any age. Young children should respond to clear directives immediately. Later, during the pre-adolescent years and beyond, a respectful, obedient child can offer some discussion: "I'll be glad to carry the papers out, Dad, but could we talk about it for a minute? I wanted to see Andy this afternoon, so could I do it tomorrow instead?" If the request is reasonable and still fits in with your overall plan, there may be no reason to deny it. But whatever the parent's response, the child should meet it with cheerful cooperation.

Third, we try to train our children to respond with humility. Allowing our children—even as they are barely learning to talk—to interrupt us or try to persuade us to change our decisions can lead to an arrogant attitude in them later. One practical way we have chosen to implement this is by having our children say "Yes, sir" or "No, ma'am" to adults. More important to us than external responses, however, is our desire to teach them to value the opinions and ideas of their family and friends over their own. Simple things like deferring to a sibling's choice of which board game to play or allowing a friend to go ahead of them in line help our children to learn the importance of esteeming others' needs as more important than theirs (Philippians 2:4).

Fourth, we require that our children show respectful attitudes toward others. We begin instructing our sons at a young age to be little gentlemen and to allow ladies to go through the door ahead of them. We encourage conversation skills like looking into the eyes of the person speaking to them; greeting those who greet them; acknowledging each comment or directive from us; and being good listeners. We also want them to be loyal to others and speak positively about their siblings and friends.

Last, we want our children to respect godly values and

standards when we are not around to enforce them. It may begin with an obedient three-year-old who refuses to go into a neighbor's backyard to play because Mommy told her to stay in her own yard, and it may result in a teenager who resists a flirtatious advance from an attractive classmate because he or she knows it could lead to a compromise of the biblical standards learned over the years. Teaching our children to stand alone against the pressures they will undoubtedly face is among Benny's and my greatest passions as parents.

Respect Involves Parental Confidence

The final ingredient of cultivating a respectful heart in our children directly involves us as parents. As I mentioned earlier, children will not respect parents who do not command this attitude from them. Yet many of us are confused as to how to require respectfulness without creating a military atmosphere.

We once heard the story of a little boy who was told by his teacher to sit in the corner for his misbehavior. "O.K.," he responded. "I just want you to know that I may be sitting down on the outside, but I'll be standing up on the inside!"

This brings to surface a common concern. We don't want our children merely to conform physically; we want their outward responses to mirror inward character. We want their *hearts* to be full of honor, love and a desire to obey. We want our relationship with them to be characterized by mutual trust.

Yet we parents undermine this process because we lack inner security and confidence. Some parents resort to yelling in order to get their children's attention and obedience. Others discipline their children in anger or frustration, thinking that this will force the child to take them more seriously. Many make threats they have little intention of carrying out to manipulate their children into responding to their directives.

Let me emphasize this: These and other wrong means of relating to children *produce the opposite of the desired effect.* They tear down rather than build up respect. Children in these situations will learn to disregard their parents' authority and lose what respect they may have had for them.

In order to have the confidence we need, we must realize that the weight of our responsibility as parents rests in our relationship with the God who entrusted the children to our care. He has both called and graced us to raise our little ones effectively. By resisting the temptation to yell, threaten or discipline in anger, we are protecting children from feeling rejected. We should explain our standards, encourage them when they respond properly, and then consistently and lovingly punish them when they disobey.

Am I suggesting that a good parent never raises his voice or struggles with frustration? Certainly not. I have had my share of failures in these areas and have had to solicit our children's forgiveness. Yet, the relationship with our children that we desire will never come about if harshness, irritation, anger, pleading and threats become the norm.

Respectful children are rare in our "children-will-be-children" world. Benny and I have seen too many cases in which respect for authority is viewed as unimportant or even undesirable. Allowing our children to live for years under our care without training them to esteem those in authority will do little to prepare them for usefulness to God.

Yes, it will also require that we discern and overcome character flaws or sinful habits that prevent us from being worthy of their respect. It will require time and energy. Yet the potential for future benefits is great. What greater thrill could a Christian parent have than seeing his or her children honor Jesus Christ and His Word above all things? This begins with helping children "practice" by honoring and respecting us.

And just think how much money we'll save on candy at the grocery store!

7
Training Children to Become Responsible

Sheree

"Is this the Phillips' home?" the telephone caller asked. "Yes, it is," Benny responded. "What can I do for you?" "I'm a neighbor down the street. I hear your son does yard work and wondered if he would be interested in raking a yard full of leaves for me. I understand he's young but I haven't been able to find any older guys who are interested."

This was one of many calls we received during the summer and fall after Joshua's eleventh birthday. We had allowed him to place his name in our neighborhood newsletter to advertise his willingness to do yard work. Many of the calls came for the same reason: People were unable to find teenage boys interested in earning pocket money by doing yard work.

When Benny told me about his latest caller we reminisced about how much Joshua had enjoyed "helping" Daddy push the lawnmower the summer after his fourth birthday. The next summer he was allowed to push the mower under Benny's watchful eye for brief periods in level areas. The following summer, at age six, he was capable enough to mow the front yard with supervision. By age seven he could mow the entire yard while Benny and I enjoyed the fruit of three summers of careful instruction! The next summer he began to mow small yards for spending money, and at age nine he earned $150 for his summer of hard work.

Several summers ago eleven-year-old Joshua decided to repeat this training process with then five-year-old Jesse. Tears brimmed in my eyes as I saw little Jesse "helping" his older brother push the mower through the yard, just as Joshua had done with Benny years earlier. Within two years Jesse was able to take on more responsibility for our lawn and release Joshua to mow neighborhood lawns and sell his handcrafted wood shelves to earn the $300 he needed to accompany Benny on a short-term missions project.

Why is it important to train our children to become responsible? A child who is trustworthy, dependable, competent and reliable also tends to have a well-developed sense of self-worth. As they are entrusted with more and more significant responsibilities in the home, and realize they are needed contributors in the family, their self-confidence grows. As their skills are then used to generate income, they learn to value and be responsible for their finances and can better appreciate and care for their belongings. Such children are prime candidates for usefulness to God who is looking for faithful men and women to whom He can entrust responsibilities in the Church (see 2 Timothy 2:2).

Teaching our children to be responsible involves not only their practical contributions to the family, but also their actions and attitudes. Before I get into the specifics of these two important areas, let's first evaluate the example we set as their parents.

Our Example

Over the years Benny and I have become aware, painfully at times, of the model we set for our children. In fact, we have had to make changes in our lives because of it. Children will usually imitate parents who leave their shoes lying wherever they pulled them off, neglect to return tools to their proper places, put the Scotch tape away in a different drawer each time they use it or forget to return borrowed items to neighbors. They also tend to duplicate the model of parents who are relationally irresponsible—refusing to admit wrong and seek others' forgiveness, not following through on commitments made to others, or talking about a problem with everyone but the person involved.

Attempts to teach our children can be frustrated by our not realizing how crucially important our example is. Instruction has a greater effect when it is accompanied by consistent demonstration. Jesus' words in Luke 6:40 can be aptly applied to the parent-child relationship: "A student is not above his teacher, but everyone who is fully trained will be like his teacher."

Let's examine ways in which we can prepare our children in both practical and relational ways for future responsibility in the Kingdom of God. Here are eight steps we can take.

The first step in training responsible children is motivating them. The easiest child to train is a willing child. We must look for ways to activate our children's desire to please us and the Lord. Because this issue is so important, we will be discussing it in depth in later chapters.

The second step we can take is to be aware of their interests. This involves capitalizing on a child's particular enthusiasm for learning a task and persevering through seasons of disinterest.

Teaching the boys to use the lawnmower involved

awareness. Four-year-old Joshua wasn't tackling the idea of ultimate responsibility for mowing the lawn on a weekly basis. He was simply eager to spend the time with his daddy and get his hands on a machine that made so much noise. We encouraged his desire to be involved in family chores by allowing him to do so.

As with any learning process, the "fun" wore off several summers later. When caring for the yard became one of his primary areas of responsibility, he didn't jump at the opportunity—especially on hot summer mornings! At times we missed his "Oh, boy, it's time to mow the lawn!" response of earlier years. We didn't expect him to maintain that excitement, and yet we didn't allow him to grumble or procrastinate when lawn-mowing day came, either.

His childlike enthusiasm of earlier summers was soon replaced, though, by a sense of fulfillment that comes from doing a job well. He would often comment about "how good it feels to stand back and look at the lawn when it's finished." This more mature attitude is also helping him learn to approach the task as a way to contribute to the family.

The third step is to encourage creativity. Most parents find that in the early years children view work as fun. Helping clean out the car or reorganize the garage is their idea of a great Saturday morning. Their enthusiasm partially comes simply from being included in their parents' world. It also comes from being too young to have been affected by others' negative attitudes about work.

Creativity enhances this perspective of enjoying work while serving Mom and Dad. Let's say, for instance, that your five-year-old asks to vacuum the living room. This is one way you, as a parent, can be alerted to your child's readiness to assume responsibility. Rather than approach him the next week with "Now, it's your responsibility to vacuum so please do it for me this morning," the creative parent may say something like, "You did such a good job vacuuming for me last week and you're becoming such a big helper, I'd like you vacuum the living room for me again." We will be getting more into this subject of chores later.

A fourth step in training responsible children is through repetition, a necessary ingredient for mastering any new skill or task. Children must be allowed to perform a particular chore over and over without heavy parental input in order to develop the self-confidence to try more difficult tasks in the future.

When our eldest daughter was young, I began to include her in various homemaking jobs, including making her bed. At eighteen months, Jaime would hand me the pillows and "help" fold the bedspread over them. At two, she would climb onto the bed and attempt to "get all the wrinkles out of the sheets." At three she was "making her bed" before breakfast.

The bedspread she had at the time had a ruffled trim that bordered the mattress. In order for the ruffle to hang properly, the border ("lines," she called them) had to be straight. When guests were coming I would often sneak into Jaime's room to straighten the lines until a disappointed Jaime suggested that I start making her bed because she wasn't doing a good enough job. No more straightening the lines!

Shortly after her fifth birthday, Jaime rushed excitedly into the kitchen. "Mommy! Mommy! Come and look! Hurry, Mommy! I got the lines straight!" I had no idea that Jaime had been trying for years to improve her bedmaking skills. There was much rejoicing at the Phillips' home that day. The years of repeating a new skill had finally paid off for a thrilled little girl.

The fifth step in instructing our children to become responsible is encouragement. Encouraging even their feeble attempts at trying a new task gives them the incentive to repeat it. Affirming their desire to help, especially in the early years when offers to help are frequent, builds a foundation that will reap benefits in later years when their assistance is both needed and greatly appreciated. Years of responding to situations like your toddler's desire to help you dust the living room by handing him a cloth of his own and saying, "Honey, thank you for offering to help Mommy. You're growing such a servant's heart!" may pave the way for a more helpful teenager in years to come.

The sixth step is clarity. Using our words and example to demonstrate our standards clearly is a vital step in training our children to become responsible. Many older children have immature skills in areas like keeping their rooms neat, cleaning the bathroom or folding the laundry because they were never instructed adequately in these tasks.

The neatness standard of their bedrooms, for example, begins first with the example set by their parents. Few children surpass their parents' own standards for neatness. Next comes their involvement with Mom or Dad in the process (for example, handing the pillows to Mommy). Soon they are making their own beds without supervision. But, of course, a neat room does not stop with making the bed. No, along the way other skills must be added like putting clothes and shoes away, dusting the furniture, vacuuming and straightening the closet and dresser drawers.

It takes time to be this clear, to communicate, teach and remind your children of your standards. Simply expecting your twelve-year-old to clean his room, becoming frustrated when he does an inadequate job, and then becoming angry or cleaning it yourself inhibits the training process.

The most effective way to be clear is by beginning at the

earliest possible age—although we have seen parents start fresh with teenage children and experience tremendous success in this area. Whatever your child's age, begin by demonstrating the standard in the care you take of your own "space." Next, invest the time in working *with* your child in his or her room—cleaning and straightening together. Little by little, make the transitions from the children watching you, to the two of you working together, to you watching him. You may even want to do something that we have found helpful for older children—posting a room-care checklist.

Clarity takes time, but it prevents the strife that comes when children do not understand our standards. It also helps us encourage their process along the way more specifically. ("Son, thank you for working so hard to straighten your toy shelf—but it looks like you forgot to check under your bed for things to put away.")

The seventh step in our children's development of responsibility is the importance of rewards. Offering something extra for a job well done goes a long way to communicate our appreciation and motivates our children to continue to grow.

We should give rewards for significant accomplishments rather than for daily responsibilities. We don't want them to think that every task earns a treat or special privilege. Yet there is a place for rewarding children for going the extra mile to serve the family or accomplishing a task they have been working hard to achieve.

The eighth and final way in which we can train responsible children is with our correction. Just as encouragement and rewards give our children incentive to repeat positive behavior, correction reminds them to *not* repeat negative behavior.

Our older children are well-schooled in the specifics of cleaning their rooms. Each has been instructed clearly about keeping his or her room neat on a daily basis as well as cleaning more thoroughly on Saturday mornings. If, for instance, I checked one of their rooms Saturday afternoon and found a shirt in the corner, I would assume it was an oversight because of the good job he or she had done on the rest of the room. I would simply place the shirt in the dirty clothes hamper. If I discovered, however, that a pile of toys or dirty socks had been "conveniently" pushed under the bed, I would call the child, affirm his or her diligence on the rest of the room and then would enforce discipline for choosing to be lazy instead of putting those things away properly. (See chapter 8: "Seeing Results Through Discipline that Works.")

Now that we have some ideas on how to train our children by our example, let's look at some practical suggestions in the two major areas mentioned earlier—responsibility for their actions and attitudes and household chores.

Actions and Attitudes

Many of us adults struggle with taking personal responsibility for our actions and attitudes. We are too quick to blame others—spouse, children, friends, boss, elected officials or even God—for our problems. Our human nature—sin nature—promotes this. Adam blamed Eve for their Fall in the Garden (Genesis 3:12). Eve then blamed the serpent (verse 13). God's response (verses 14–19) showed that those involved—Adam, Eve and the serpent—were personally responsible for their decisions. Each, therefore, had to suffer individual consequences for his or her disobedience.

We are, likewise, each accountable to God for the ways we respond to various challenges and temptations. Maybe your boss's frustration because you couldn't complete a project in an unrealistic amount of time was unfair, yet your decision to let this produce moodiness and self-pity in you, affecting the time with your family that evening, was equally unfair.

Just as adults must take personal responsibility, so we must teach our children that they cannot blame others for their misbehavior or wrong attitudes. Their tendency to lie or minimize their offenses must be addressed.

Children should learn from an early age to admit they were wrong. They should learn to feel comfortable saying, "I'm sorry," "I was the one who turned the television on without asking," or, "I grabbed the toy from my sister." The humility that comes from taking personal responsibility in these ways in the early years lays the foundation for strong character development.

Household Chores

The second area in which we can train our children to be responsible is in their practical contributions in the home. Many parents find the demands of parenting and keeping an orderly home exhausting because of uncooperative, lazy children. These youngsters think Mom and Dad are there to serve them and feel no responsibility to the family. How many mothers of older children, even teenagers, still perform the majority of the housework?

Requiring children to do chores produces much more than a tidy home. It also makes them feel like vitally needed members of the family and increases their appreciation of their parents' work. Plus it teaches them dependability, thoroughness and patience.

I would like to mention the subject of allowances here, too. Many parents give their children a weekly allowance as compensation for household chores. Some, in fact, give more allowance certain weeks when the children take on greater responsibilities. They withhold the allowance, conversely, as an incentive for completing their chores. The implication is that a child who doesn't pull his weight in the home during the week shouldn't have the privilege of getting an allowance on Friday.

Benny and I have come to view the allowance differently. We wonder if a child who sees his allowance as a reward for completing household chores might not presume that the decision to perform or not perform his responsibilities in the home is his. In a given week he may decide that he would rather forego his allowance than do his chores. He may also begin to equate work in the home with financial reimbursement. Soon he expects to be rewarded for any extra help. When he has a special need for money, he is unusually helpful; otherwise, he returns to his more normal passive self.

Our philosophy of allowance relates to family togetherness. Each family member has responsibilities, jobs that help make the home run smoothly and function peacefully (especially with the size of our family!). Because we each share in the responsibilities, we also each share in the privileges, one of which is finances.

How do you determine when your child is ready to begin receiving a weekly allowance? You may want to ask yourself these three questions:

1. Is he/she participating regularly in the family responsibilities without needing constant reminders? Waiting until this time helps to prevent money from becoming the incentive to participate rather than a desire to serve the family.

2. Is he/she mature enough to learn some initial money management principles (saving, tithing, blessing others) vs. wanting to make a trip to the toy store every Friday?

3. Could he/she continue to perform household chores cheerfully if unexpected financial changes meant a temporary withholding of the allowance?

If your answer to these questions is yes, your child is probably ready for an allowance. This usually happens between ages five and ten. When explaining it to him or her, you might consider something like this: "Dad and Mom are so grateful for the way you serve in the home. You are becoming very responsible and helpful. Because you are sharing so many of the responsibilities that help our home run smoothly, you are now going to begin sharing in the money that God blesses us with." You can then communicate the amount and discuss the importance of saving, tithing, setting aside money to bless others and "fun money" for spending.

Over the years of teaching on the subject of training children to become responsible, Benny and I have found that many parents appreciate ideas about appropriate chores for different age levels. The following suggestions are dependent on the individual child's verbal and motor development in the early years.

In reading through this listing, you may notice that your nine-year-old is barely performing the tasks listed under age three. Don't be discouraged! This list assumes early implementation. Simply begin where your child is currently—no matter what age is suggested—and then progress from that point. These recommendations cover only the early childhood years. Adaptation can be made for later years as needed.

Stages of Responsibility

9–12 months
- Beginning to help collect and place toys in proper place.
- When words begin, attempting to say "please" and "thank you."

1–2 years
- Putting dirty clothes in hamper.
- "Helping" with grocery shopping (putting items in basket, carrying light items into the house, handing things to Mom to put away).
- Helping clean (empty Windex bottle, dust rag, child-sized broom).
- Watering plants (with pre-measured amounts!).
- Beginning to help make beds.
- Yard work (helping collect trash, toys).
- Simple errands (diaper for the baby, garbage into the trash).

2–3 years
- Requiring politeness on a regular basis ("O.K., Mommy," "May I be excused from the table?" as language develops).
- Generally including child in everyday activities (cleaning, shopping, some meal preparations).
- More complicated errands in the home.
- Laundry (beginning to learn sorting procedure by handing items to put into appropriate piles, transferring clothes from washer to dryer to basket).
- Learning more specific neatness qualities (putting toys in proper places).
- Taking dishes to the sink after meals and helping to clear the table (trash, plastic items, silverware).
- Carrying groceries in from the car, Mom's purse into the store, diaper bag for the baby.
- Simple decision-making ("Would you like juice or milk?").

3–4 years
- Making bed with help.
- Keeping room neat and taking daily responsibility for it.

- Regular morning routine of dressing, straightening room, helping set the table for breakfast.
- More complex decision-making ("Would you like to wear the blue shorts or the white ones?").
- Becoming "others-oriented" (drawing pictures for someone who is sick, drawing "thank you" pictures for birthday presents from others, dictating notes for others).
- Learning to use the telephone properly (begin with toy telephone for practice).
- Regular chores (getting the mail, emptying bathroom wastebaskets, feeding pets).
- Helping wash the car.
  [Note: At this point you may notice your child enjoying being a contributor to the home, talking about what he/she can do, offering to do more complex things.]

4–5 years
- Taking his laundry to designated place on laundry day.
- Sorting laundry with supervision.
- Beginning to learn to fold laundry (towels, small items).
- Vacuuming/sweeping.
- Cleaning table after meals.
- Helping with meal preparations (learning to measure, stir and use simple appliances with *much* supervision).
- Setting the table.
- Taking out the trash.
- Helping Dad mow the lawn.
  [Note: At this point your efforts as parents are beginning to pay off as their help is now really helpful!]

5–6 years
- Unsupervised responsibilities (making bed, washing out garbage cans).
- More complicated meal preparations (helping to make sandwiches, toast, scrambling eggs with supervision, cutting with blunt knife).

- Helping with younger siblings (learning to change diapers, helping with bath, entertaining while parent is out of the room, feeding/helping to dress toddler siblings).
- Laundry (sorting, learning to use washer/dryer, measuring detergent).
- Cleaning (using some supplies, dusting furniture, cleaning bathtub).
- Carrying groceries in with parents and helping to put them away.
- Beginning usage of lawn mower with direct supervision.
  [Note: By this time your child may begin to carry out responsibilities unasked, especially when he or she is regularly thanked/encouraged.]

6–7 years
- Simple meal preparations (making lunch sandwiches, juice, salad for dinner, scrambled eggs and toast).
- Totally unsupervised laundry responsibilities when needed.
- Loading/unloading the dishwasher.
- Increased responsibilities for younger siblings (dressing infants and young toddlers, entertaining for longer periods, reading books to them). Children who feel needed and appreciated are less tempted to resent this.
- Learning the purpose and beginning usage of tools and being included in home maintenance.
- Partial lawn-mowing responsibilities.

8–10 years
- Complete responsibility for his/her room (maintenance and thorough cleaning).
- Unsupervised yard work (mowing, edging, cleanup, etc.).
- More complex meal preparations (using sharper instruments, baking, using appliances, beginning meal planning).
- More difficult cleaning projects (scrubbing kitchen floor, windows, cleaning appliances).
- Summer jobs (mowing lawns, walking dogs, daytime babysitting, odd jobs for vacationers).

- Financial planning.
- Beginning car maintenance (helping with minor repairs, washing/waxing, usage and handling of tools).

Whew! You may be wondering if this is all possible. Can children really be trained to contribute to the family as suggested above? Is the child, who at age ten is relatively untrained in household responsibilities, really going to change?

We mentioned that my sister, Bonnie, became the single mother of two young children. As her younger, Doug, approached the teenage years, she realized she had not instructed him effectively in areas of personal and household responsibilities. Benny and I agreed to help begin guiding Doug in this area. By age fourteen, unlike the majority of his peers, Doug had become responsible enough to babysit for our four young children under the age of seven.

Benny and I benefitted from the fruit of our labors with our children in the winter of 1986. We had found recently that we were expecting our fifth child. At ages eight, six-and-a-half and almost three, our older children were thrilled. Eight weeks into the pregnancy complications occurred that threatened a miscarriage. I was told to confine myself to bed for, we hoped, a few days. Friends from the church responded by providing meals and helping to care for the four children. Yet, after a week, the problem still existed.

Another visit to the doctor confirmed the need for further bedrest until the complications were resolved. The only alternative was to risk losing the baby. Friends continued to bring meals for several weeks and Benny took off time from work as his schedule allowed, yet the biggest part of the responsibility fell on young Joshua and Jaime.

During what became a five-week period of bedrest, they potty-trained Jesse ("Jaime, quick, get him to the bathroom!

Yea! Jesse, you did it!"), washed most of the laundry, made lunches, entertained and cared for thirteen-month-old Joey, maintained a heroic level of neatness in the home and took lots of telephone messages. They even checked lovingly to see if I needed anything to drink or wanted someone to read a story to me.

It was an extremely emotional time for us. Watching our young children have to take on so much responsibility was difficult, and yet they rose to the challenge. Fearing the loss of our baby was the only incentive I had to cooperate with the unusual demands our children were experiencing.

In early September we were all able to enjoy the fruit of those winter weeks of stress and turmoil when Janelle Marie was born. As Benny and I stood with our four children at the hospital window, and they admired their new little sister, we were struck with the real realization of their part in our being able to share that moment.

"Joshua and Jaime," Benny said, "we want you to know that we have you to thank for this special day. Because of your servants' hearts and willingness to take such good care of Mommy when she had to stay in bed, we now have a new little sister. Part of the reason she is here today is because of you!"

The tears we shared that day are a permanent part of our memories and began a wonderful relationship between the two older children and their new sister.

The goal of raising responsible children is not simply to have help keeping the house clean and the laundry done, as meaningful as this is. As parents our ultimate ambition must be to raise children who, having been trained to be responsible in the natural, can be entrusted with spiritual responsibilities by the God who has a call of service in His Kingdom for each of their lives. However that call comes to serve Him and others—whether as a carpenter, homemaker, lawyer, pastor or schoolteacher—He has promised that those who have been faithful with a few things in this life will be given greater responsibility (Matthew 25:21).

Dependable, trustworthy, reliable young people offer a rich testimony of God's grace to a watching world. The selfishness, worldliness and "serve-me" mentality of today's young generation can be affected most by a counterculture of unselfish young people who delight in serving others. Will this happen because we pray hard and take them to a church building every Sunday? That will certainly help. Yet the best way to see our little ones emerge into adulthood primed for successful handling of their responsibilities as spouses, parents, employees, friends and participants in advancing God's Kingdom will be because they were trained to be faithful with a few things.

Are we suggesting that the child who simply learns to clean his or her room at age seven will eventually have a place of responsibility in the Kingdom of God? Certainly not. There are many other factors that will influence his or her spiritual development. Nevertheless, we have seen that training our children to become responsible, hard-working members of their families, when coupled with other factors, has produced tremendous results.

Little Janelle would agree.

8
Fostering a Responsive Heart

Sheree

We have discussed two significant building blocks in preparing our children for the future—respect and responsibility. The final essential ingredient in cultivating their hunger for God is responsiveness in three important areas: responsiveness to us as their parents, responsiveness to others and, most importantly, responsiveness to God.

Why is responsiveness such an important issue in our children's present and future relationship with the Lord? Remember, whatever we train them to do in the "natural" will ultimately affect the "spiritual." Children who are encouraged to respond properly to their parents and others will be better primed to have a responsive heart toward God.

Jason is the young son of some close friends. During his toddler years he tended to be somewhat shy and lacking in confidence. His parents were sensitive to Jason's being more introverted than his two older siblings, but refused to accept his immature social skills as "just the way he is." Over the years they required him to establish eye contact with those to whom he was speaking, to greet people cheerfully and to respond with more than yes or no when engaged in conversation by others.

At eight years old, Jason is a different boy. Now, his warm greetings make others feel loved and special. Being trained to be responsive to those close to him has begun to affect his responsiveness to others as well.

We were recently together as families—Larry and Doris with their four children and us with our six. While walking together near a busy city street, attempting to keep all our "ducks in a row," we noticed Jason lagging behind the group. We watched as he pulled something from his pocket. He then approached a homeless man who was sitting on a nearby bench. He spoke briefly to the man, handed him something and jogged away to join the group.

"Jason," Doris asked, "what were you doing?"

"I wanted to give that man a tract, Mommy. I bet he doesn't know Jesus and I asked him to read it."

We all affirmed Jason for his compassion and courage. This kind of loving responsiveness was nurtured by parents who saw the need to train their son in little ways in the early years to help him shed self-consciousness and become others-conscious. He had not been permitted to withdraw from others, hide behind Mommy when greeted or avoid interacting with people. His parents' training gave him the concern and boldness to reach out to a lonely stranger in need of God's love.

We can envision how these qualities could affect Jason's relationship with God. The tenderness and unselfishness that he is learning by relating properly to his parents and others will help prepare him for a similar responsiveness to the Lord. A child who has learned to respond to others eagerly is better equipped to respond to God—in worship, devotion and abandonment to His call.

As Christian parents, we pray fervently that our children

develop an intimate relationship with God. Few things would bring us more joy than seeing them participate in an expressive, loving alliance with Jesus Christ. How can we do our part to foster the kind of responsiveness that will help our prayers become reality?

Responsiveness to Parents

The first way we can cultivate this quality in our children is by teaching them to respond properly to us as their parents.

Behavior patterns like respect for authority, honesty, study and work habits, and patience can be established in the early stages of a child's life. Such qualities are especially important to focus on in the years before children are exposed regularly to the values and standards of others—that is, before they start school.

This is not to say that parents who get a later start won't be successful. On the contrary, we have seen many parents who were willing to be patient and consistent experience tremendous results with older children. Nevertheless, the earlier we begin the more opportunity we have for success. Like Larry and Doris, we must help our children react appropriately in "little ways" in the early years. By doing so, we are training them to develop a tender and responsive heart toward God.

You may be thinking, "Well, what about me? My parents didn't make me look into others' eyes and greet them when I was three, and I have a great relationship with God! Aren't you taking this a little too far?"

Like you, I am grateful that God is able to invade our lives—despite the way we were raised—to pursue a relationship with us. His redemptive mercy has nothing to do with who we are or how our parents trained us. Still, as parents we have the amazing ability to help prepare our children for usefulness to God by the way we teach, instruct, discipline and train them. This process may well protect them from having to deal with the kinds of character deficiencies we find ourselves still struggling with.

Look at some of our responses as adults:

"God, why did You allow me to marry this person?"

"Why haven't You provided another job for me? I can't take this boss much longer!"

"Why do I have to go to her to resolve our differences? After all, she's the one who offended *me!*"

"How can You expect me to give money to the church? I'm having a hard enough time as it is!"

"God, I can't reach out to my unbelieving neighbors and family members. Evangelism just isn't my ministry!"

Whether it's through studying the Bible, hearing a sermon, talking with a friend or spending time in prayer, we are receiving regular "messages" from God that require responses. If you are like me, too often the responses are arguments and complaints.

As we think through all the reasons why we are unqualified, unable or unwilling to comply with God's standards or directives, we can often trace them to a lack of training in childhood. Whether outwardly or inwardly, we allowed ourselves to resist or rebel against our parents' authority. We learned to react rather than respond. As adults, we now find ourselves relating similarly to God.

I mentioned earlier that when given a direct command, children should *respond* rather than *react:*

"Jesse, it's your turn to load the dishwasher after dinner."

"O.K., Daddy."

"Josh, would you please straighten up the carport before Daddy comes home?"

"Sure, Mom."

"Jaime, it would really help if you would give the baby a bath while I fold some laundry."

"I'd be glad to, Mommy."

These kinds of answers from our older children have come after years of correcting reactions like "Do I have to do it now?" or "I want to finish my puzzle." It begins with not allowing your two-year-old to pout and whine when it's time for bed or your three-year-old to argue with your decision that it's time to leave the playground.

Purely motivated parental love that seeks the *best* for the child is the kind of foundation that will help our children to want to cooperate with us. This kind of love says yes *and* no. Love without standards produces a selfish, spoiled child. Standards without love produce a broken, discouraged child.

God's love resulted in giving. He gave that which was the most precious to Him—His Son (John 3:16). His love in us prevents us from comparing our children to others and is full of grace and patience (Proverbs 16:32, 17:27). Crying out to God for the unconditional love we need for our children will lead to wisdom, courage and consistency to exercise loving authority in their lives. More will be discussed about this in the next chapter on discipline.

Responsiveness to Others

As our children learn to respond to us cheerfully and willingly, we can train them to do likewise with others. You may wonder how legitimate it is to expect this of children with varying personalities. Some children, for example, are more naturally extroverted and social while others are not. Requiring the same standard of all children may seem unrealistic and unfair.

With six children, Benny and I can easily identify with this line of thinking. We are very aware that even children from the same family are distinctively different in personality and temperament. They have the same parents but couldn't be more different in their social abilities. Yet we have found that even the most introverted child can be trained to grow in warmth and confidence in responding to others.

At eleven our daughter Jaime is a friendly and cooperative young lady. She enjoys being with people, greets individuals warmly and is known for her cheerful telephone manner. She serves confidently at the hospitalities in our home, often welcoming our friends at the door. Whether with adults, small children or peers, Jaime is learning to interact with others with poise and graciousness.

Years ago this was only hopeful thinking for our little girl. Although she has always had a sweet disposition, she was insecure around others. Around the age of two, she began to display excessive shyness—looking away when others greeted her, refusing to say hello or running to her room when visitors came.

Rather than accept the advice of some who suggested this was normal two-year-old behavior, we remembered those parents whose older children had never "grown out of" this kind of behavior. We began to discipline Jaime for being unresponsive to others. At home we would role-play social situations with her.

"Jaime, let's pretend we're at the grocery store and I'm the checker who says hello to you. Show Mommy how you should respond."

I also made a chart for the refrigerator with a dozen or so squares. Every time she responded to someone properly she received a happy-face sticker to put into one square. When the chart was full she was rewarded with a trip to the ice cream store.

Over the months we saw wonderful results. My expectation was not that Jaime should become the "life-of-the-party" person that God didn't create her to be. Yet I was unwilling to wait and simply hope that she would grow into poise and confidence in her relationships with others.

Selfishness is our children's greatest enemy in the quest for responsiveness to others. They are not born desiring to bless and serve others. On the contrary, they consider their own needs, wants and ideas as being paramount. They must be trained to think differently.

How can we do this?

First, we can cultivate compassionate hearts in our children. Simple things like taking cookies to a new neighbor, making Christmas cards for an elderly "grandma" down the street or praying for the person in a passing ambulance begins to alert our children to the needs of others. Modeling a heart of love for unbelievers by praying for and sharing the Gospel with them helps to cultivate evangelistic awareness and courage in them. Years of such expressions of compassion—especially to those we may not feel naturally drawn to—will foster loving attitudes.

Second, we can cultivate sensitivity. We can train our children, by our actions and example, to have concern for the poor, handicapped and elderly. We know one couple in ministry with a very full life who often take their adolescent daughters to serve in a soup kitchen for the poor. Another mother and daughter regularly visit the nursing home in their area to reach out to elderly folks who have few visitors. This helps our children bring their own needs and wants into perspective.

Third, we can cultivate responsiveness through politeness. Politeness should become characteristic of our children—learning to say things like, "May I have that toy when you're finished with it?" rather than "Gimme that! I want a turn!"

Finally, we can cultivate the importance of flexibility. A child's wrong reaction to others is often based on his feeling his "rights" have been violated—his right to watch a certain television program or play a certain board game; his right to stay longer at a friend's house or sleep late; his right to free time or a snack before dinner. Children can and should be taught to adapt to undesired situations with flexibility.

Again, our parental example is so vital. How do you react to similar violations of your perceived "rights"? Your husband remembers he made an appointment to get the car brakes checked just as you're about to drive off to the mall. Your wife reminds you of your promise to install the bathroom carpet just as you realize it's time for the football game on television to begin. For the fourth time in an hour, your four-year-old wants a drink of water while you're trying to make headway with the laundry that is taking over your basement. The model we provide *for* our children in such situations either validates or jeopardizes the standard we expect *from* them.

How we need the grace of God! Like me, you may be personally in the midst of being "trained" by the Holy Spirit in these areas. Your responses—or should I say "reactions"—leave much to be desired. And yet, you see that the responsibility is yours to teach your children that which you have yet to master!

Relax. Benny and I identify easily with your plight. We have a certain "look" we exchange discreetly between ourselves when the way in which we react to a situation is a poor example to the children. Under certain circumstances, especially with our older children, we acknowledge our bad attitudes and ask their forgiveness for being a wrong example to them. In other situations we simply appreciate the reminder from a caring spouse. Each couple must decide what's appropriate for them in various situations.

Like you, I am well aware of areas of character weakness in my life. I battle the temptation to react selfishly to inconvenient requests. I frequently miss opportunities to express concern and compassion for others. I'm certainly not always flexible when my plans must change in deference to others. Like you, though, I want to build a heart of servanthood and unselfishness in myself and in our children. A heart that is compassionate, sensitive, considerate and flexible. A heart that is fertile ground for usefulness to God.

Responsiveness to God

Working on these first two areas—training our children to have an attentive heart to us and to others—will result in responsiveness to God.

Do you desire your children to have a strong relationship with the Lord? Do you want them to resist the self-consciousness and vanity that leads to apathetic praise and worship? Do you have aspirations for their usefulness to God in ministry—whether in service to the church or in the business world? Do you long for them to be ready to hear and obey God's voice?

Surely your answer to these questions is a resounding yes! Seeing our children mature in these ways begins with a simple truth: They must be taught to respond to God. This means to respond to His pursuit of them; to respond to opportunities to serve and reach out to those He puts on their hearts; to respond to childlike desires to talk about Jesus with their friends; and to respond to opportunities to give their dimes and quarters to the church building project.

Benny and I are still learning to allow our children the privilege of responding to God. There was the time when then eight-year-old Joshua wanted to start the "Phillips Evangelism Club" in our carport. He made a sign from an old cardboard box and informed the neighborhood children of his desire to talk about Jesus with them. He and Jaime sought to convince our wonderfully cross-cultural neighborhood children with various religious backgrounds of their need for a relationship with Jesus. Our decision to risk being misunderstood by our neighbors for the sake of cultivating our children's responsiveness to God bore good fruit. One prayed to receive Jesus while sitting in a tree with Josh and no neighbors expressed any concern over our zealous young evangelists!

Then there was the time when young Joshua came and said he thought Jesus wanted to help his grandmother quit smoking. Our five-year-old took on his nearly sixty-year-old grandmother who had been smoking for more than thirty years and had little desire to stop. He told her the Lord wanted her to stop smoking. As a Christian, she appreciated his concern and agreed that smoking was an unhealthy habit. Each time he saw her—which was often—Josh reminded her that he was praying for her. Year after year he asked her to quit smoking and even hid her cigarettes at times. When he prayed before meals he would often end with, "And please help Nannie to quit smoking." When, at age ten, he used $25 of his own money to purchase a mail-order system guaranteed to help smokers kick the habit, Nannie couldn't take it anymore. She is now a non-smoker!

A meaningful opportunity to encourage our children's sensitivity to God happened several years ago. Joshua and Benny were invited to attend a basketball game with some friends. Rather than charge an admission fee, the school where the game was held decided to ask spectators to bring used or new toys for distribution to needy families for Christmas.

Jaime joined the excitement. She and her brother needed to choose two toys—one for Benny's admission and one for Joshua's—to donate. We encouraged them to ask Jesus to help them make an unselfish choice and to choose nice toys that weren't broken or tattered. When they emerged from their bedrooms with their choices, we were surprised. They had both chosen their favorite toys—Jaime's doll and Joshua's stuffed bear—to give. Benny and I exchanged glances, wondering if their choices were wise. Both toys had been expensive gifts from relatives. Our concern for how those givers might feel, coupled—we discovered later—with an unexpected hesitance to give away something so "nice," caused us to pause. Yet, fortunately, we both recognized this as another opportunity to affirm our children's hearts for God's way and praised them for their unselfishness. (Isn't it amazing how frequently we find ourselves learning from *them!*)

Commitment to these principles is costly. It requires regular discipline, encouragement and instruction. It requires interrupting their sibling arguments to correct and teach proper responses. It requires training—day after day after day—on how to answer politely, respectfully, cheerfully and willingly to us and to others.

Mostly, however, it requires faith. Faith when we become discouraged at their lack of progress. Faith during seasons when they slip back into old habits. Faith when we realize we have started to allow arguing and bickering and anger back into our homes and we have to regroup. Faith when well-meaning friends and family say our standards are unrealistically high. Faith when we're tired and think it was easier when we didn't have to do so much disciplining and encouraging and reminding.

The apostle Paul offers us both a sober warning and a thrilling promise in Galatians 6:7–9:

> Do not be deceived: God cannot be mocked. A man reaps what he sows. The one who sows to please his sinful nature, from that nature will reap destruction; the one who sows to please the Spirit, from the Spirit will reap eternal life. Let us not become weary in doing good, for at the proper time we will reap a harvest *if we do not give up.*

The faith we need to persevere can come only from God. Our children will be uncooperative at times. Their progress in overcoming selfish habits and disrespectful attitudes may be slow. Nevertheless, our long-term goal of cultivating their responsiveness to God can keep us going when unbelief comes knocking at the door. Weariness is often a symptom of trying to accomplish God's will on our own without His energy, wisdom and anointing.

Benny and I try to take time to evaluate ourselves in this crucial area on a regular basis. Are we maintaining a standard of respect? Are we correcting their wrong behavior consistently? Are we encouraging their obedience and progress? Are we modeling the standards we expect from them in our relationship as a couple? Is our relationship with the Lord characterized by the kind of responsiveness and zeal we desire to see in them?

Asking ourselves difficult questions like these can be convicting. We may have to realign our standards and make a fresh commitment to God and one another. Fortunately, the sowing and reaping process always produces results. As we parents are faithful to do our part to train our children, God is faithful to bless us with the fruit of our labor. You may be feeling weary even now. Maybe you are overwhelmed at the changes you need to make. Remember, the faith you need is abundantly available from the One who has both called and equipped you with grace for the task of parenting. Any mistakes you have made can be forgiven and redeemed for your good. Evaluate areas of lack and then begin the "sowing" process.

I can't promise you success, but God has promised that you will reap good results in due season as you commit yourself to hearing from and responding to Him. Your example will go a long way in training your children to do the same.

9
Seeing Results Through Discipline that Works

Benny

Discipline. For most of us, the word itself produces negative thoughts—structure, boundaries, restrictions, spankings, lost privileges. Perhaps even thoughts of harshness and anger come to mind.

Sheree and I have met few adults who were raised by parents who disciplined them lovingly and consistently. Some were punished by frustrated parents who, after trying various means of coercion, resorted to spanking in anger. For others, corporal punishment was seldom used and they were allowed to get by with attitudes and behavior they are now unwilling to tolerate in their own children. Tragically, others were slapped, pushed, shouted at or beaten.

It's no wonder that child discipline is a difficult topic of consideration. In reaction to the ineffective or harsh means with which our generation was disciplined, today's parents find themselves shrinking from this important aspect of parenting. Fearing that we may duplicate the mistakes of our parents, we muddle through—hoping our children will turn out O.K.

Why is it that children need discipline? To punish them for irritating behavior? Teach them who is "boss" in the family? Convince them to do what they've been told? The humble parent will admit to the temptation of thinking of these and other inappropriate reasons.

Discipline is an important factor in our children's lives for several significant reasons. It helps expose them to their sin natures and, thus, their need for a Savior. It gives them the security of parental love and protection. It leads them out of selfishness, foolishness and rebellion and into conformity with Jesus Christ. It helps to develop their character and enables them to interact well with others. The most important fruit of discipline, however, is that it equips our children to accept and mature from the discipline that will eventually come from God.

Becoming an adult doesn't mark the end of our need for discipline. Plane schedules "discipline" us to arrive at the airport on time. Audits and fines "discipline" us to report our earnings. As Christians, God "disciplines" us by using various circumstances, hardships or consequences of sin to cause maturity and conformity to Christ.

Notice these words from the author of Hebrews:

> "My son, do not make light of the Lord's discipline, and do not lose heart when he rebukes you, because the Lord disciplines those he loves, and he punishes everyone he accepts as a son." Endure hardship as disci-

pline; God is treating you as sons. For what son is not disciplined by his father? If you are not disciplined (and everyone undergoes discipline), then you are illegitimate children and not true sons.... No discipline seems pleasant at the time, but painful. Later on, however, it produces a harvest of righteousness and peace for those who have been trained by it.

Hebrews 12:5–8, 11

Do you struggle with maturing during those events, challenges and hardships that God uses to discipline you? Do you find yourself tempted to become bitter and confused about why God has allowed certain things to happen to you? Do you refuse to be comforted by knowing He desires to use them for your good? Do you find yourself struggling with sinful behavior and attitudes, even after years of walking with God?

Responding affirmatively to these questions indicates a lack of understanding of the discipline of the Lord. You may not even realize that you have received God's discipline. In recent years, Christianity has been inundated with the "bless me, Lord" mentality that focuses overly on God's provision and mercy to the neglect of a rightful emphasis on His holiness. Many of us, consequently, don't discern our need for the kind of maturity that comes through God's discipline. We can, therefore, miss an important aspect of fulfilling His call on our lives.

In his book *Knowing God*, J. I. Packer addresses this correlation between the discipline of God and our future destiny:

> [Christians] know that holiness is their Father's will for them, and that it is both a means, condition, and constituent of their happiness, here and hereafter; and because they love their Father they actively seek the

fulfilling of His beneficent purpose. Paternal discipline exercised through outward pressure and trials helps the process along; the Christian up to his eyes in trouble can take comfort from the knowledge that in God's kindly plan it all has a positive purpose, to further his sanctification. In this world, royal children have to undergo training and discipline, which other children escape, in order to fit them for their high destiny. It is the same with the children of the King of kings. The clue to understanding all His dealings with them is to remember that throughout their lives He is training them for what awaits them, and chiseling them into the image of Christ.

What a visionary way to approach the concept of discipline! By understanding this kind of eternal perspective we can learn to embrace more fully the discipline of the Lord *and* to fulfill more consistently the responsibility of disciplining our own children.

Can you begin to see the way in which these two principles are related? Children who learn to embrace and not resent their parents' discipline will be more attuned to the discipline of the Lord.

Does this mean our children should leap for joy at the prospect of being disciplined? Of course not. As the writer of Hebrews says, discipline is painful. No one healthy invites pain. Yet, year after year of loving, consistent discipline can protect them from having the purely negative perspective about it that many of us struggle with.

As a conscientious Christian parent you undoubtedly desire to make wise decisions about the important place of discipline in your children's lives. To do so, you must ask yourself five foundational questions:

1. Do I desire to become better aware of what the Bible says about child discipline?

2. Am I willing to respond to God's direction in this area, even if this requires changing my disciplinary practices?

3. Am I willing to stand alone in what I feel God is saying to me about child discipline—even if family, friends or child-rearing experts disagree with my decisions?

4. Am I willing to deal with personal character flaws and sins that would prevent me from implementing a biblical approach to disciplining my children?

5. Am I willing to invest the time and consistency needed for child discipline?

If your answers to the above questions are yes, you are ready to consider ways in which the disciplinary practices in your home can be enhanced. You may need to consider how your attitudes toward this aspect of childrearing have been affected harmfully by your upbringing. Negative memories could prevent you from having the confidence and conviction you need to discipline your children. Or you may need to evaluate areas in which you have been overly affected by the advice of the newest "expert" the women's magazines are quoting. Or you may have to reestablish your conviction that the Bible is the ultimate authority in all that you do as a Christian—including discipline.

I cannot possibly exhaust the subject of discipline in one chapter. Many individuals have done the hard work of serving the Christian community with books in this area. I will restrict our discussion to the most commonly asked questions Sheree and I have received about discipline over the years. I submit these responses for your consideration from our experience and that of the many parents with whom we have been privileged to interact.

Most Commonly Asked Questions

I have narrowed our most frequently asked inquiries into the seven questions below. I hope these answers will serve in your personal pursuit of God's perspective on discipline.

1. *What is the most effective way to discipline young children?*

Do you remember the first time you laid your sweet, happy baby down on the bed to change a diaper and were met with screaming, kicking and squirming to get away? How about the time you had to leave a restaurant in frustration because your toddler was standing in the high chair, crying to get down and throwing his food onto the floor? At some point, all parents begin to realize that the adorable baby they brought home from the hospital is not always going to respond to "Honey, please don't do that."

Confused and eager to learn ways to deal with our child's temper or irritating behavior, we turn to friends, books, magazines or our own upbringing to find answers. But the conflicting advice—reason with them, ignore them, distract them, confine them to their rooms, try everything and then spank them—leaves us more confused than ever.

There is, of course, only one source in which we Christians can put our trust: God's Word. We have faith, for instance, that because the Bible says Jesus Christ lived a sinless life, died in payment for our sins and rose victoriously over death, we can become a part of His Kingdom and be reconciled to God. We have given our lives to this truth.

In a similar way, we must trust what the Bible has to say about child discipline. Experts change their minds, but God's Word will stand when all else fails.

What, then, does the Bible say about how to discipline our children? The Bible clearly calls for using the "rod of correction" or spanking. Notice a few of the many verses on this subject from the book of Proverbs:

He who spares the rod hates his son, but he who loves him is careful to discipline him.   13:24

Folly is bound up in the heart of a child, but the rod of discipline will drive it far from him.   22:15

The rod of correction imparts wisdom, but a child left to itself disgraces his mother.   29:15

In his book *God, the Rod, and Your Child's Bod*, Larry Tomczak refers to spanking as "the art of loving correction." He stresses that disciplining our children should always be done in the presence of a strong love bond between the child and his or her parent(s). Disciplining our children in anger is detrimental rather than helpful to their character development and spiritual hunger.

We have found that disciplining with the rod (that is, a neutral object) is the most effective way to train children out of negative behavior and attitudes. First, because it is clearly biblical and, second, because it works.

Punishment, unlike disciplining with the rod, deprives the child of some privilege or reward but does not deal effectively with the issues of the heart—their selfishness, rebellion, deceitfulness or unkindness. Punishment alone, therefore, leaves the child feeling frustrated or even bitter rather than helping him overcome the guilt of his offense and be hesitant to repeat it.

Contrary to popular secular thought, spanking done by loving parents does not produce insecure children who fear their parents' wrath. Rather, it can produce happy and obedient children who enjoy the security of clearly defined standards and a well-developed sense of self-worth.

2. *Who is responsible for administering the discipline?*

In many homes, one parent becomes the primary disciplinarian. While it is normal for one parent to be more aware of areas of needed correction in the children, we have found it harmful for one parent to be overly involved. At best it could make the children become more responsive (that is, obedient, cooperative) to the "spanking" parent. At worst it could make children alienate themselves from the "stricter" parent and lose respect for the more lenient one.

Spanking should be done by both parents. Colossians 3:20 instructs children to obey their *parents* in all things. This means that if Mom has been with the kids all day she should not wait for Dad to come home to spank the misbehavers. It means that Dad should take the initiative when he might rather read the paper.

3. *For what reasons do you spank?*

This is a difficult question to answer because all parents should prayerfully develop their own criteria for spanking. Relying on someone else's guidelines can result in a lack of consistency and faith to experience lasting results. I offer the following suggestions for your consideration, therefore, hoping that you will discuss them as a couple and seek God about how you might implement them in your home.

- Willful disobedience—When your child chooses to disobey a clear command ("Please put your toys away"). I am not speaking of childish occurrences like carelessly spilling milk or accidentally breaking something.
- Improper attitudes—Displaying selfishness or anger,

especially in their relationships with others (grab-bing, refusing to share, screaming, pouting).

- Disrespect—Refusing to relate to you and others with kindness, humility and responsiveness (arguing, interrupting rudely, purposely throwing/breaking things, using unkind names or faces to hurt others).
- Lying—Refusing to admit or take responsibility for their words, actions or attitudes.
- Hurting others—Using either physical or emotional means to hurt others (purposely hitting, biting, kick-ing, pushing, name-calling, belittling).

These standards must be understood clearly by the chil-dren. They shouldn't be surprised by an unexpected swat on the leg or yank on the arm for something they have been allowed to get away with in the past. Children should be taught at an early age the rules and the consequences they face when those rules are broken.

4. *What is the procedure for spanking?*

For a spanking to be effective, it must be an "event." It should take time. A frustrated slap on the leg, accompa-nied by a harsh rebuke, is an ineffective way to curb a child's wrong behavior or attitude. This is especially true when they are corrected for the same behavior that was unaddressed the day (or minute!) before and may go un-addressed tomorrow.

Clear Beginning. The first step in the spanking process is to make sure your child understands why he is receiving the spanking. Nothing will embitter him more than being con-fused about why he is being disciplined. This does not mean he has to agree that the spanking is deserved ("But Mommy, he *made* me hit him because he grabbed my toy!"). He must simply be made aware of the standard that has been vio-lated.

Many parents find that the spanking process needs to begin around age one, when children start disobeying the simple commands and are regularly displaying negative attitudes. At this age, of course, their understanding of the directives can be hard to ascertain. Remember, though, that children comprehend things long before they can talk about them. Even our one-year-old, Jacob, knows to glance around to see if we are watching him when he crawls toward a forbidden plant or deliberately throws his Cheerios on the floor.

Immediacy. The spanking should be administered as soon as possible. Children under age two have an especially short attention span and will forget what they did to warrant being disciplined. This requires a commitment to take the necessary steps (stopping the car on the side of the road, being aware of the location of restrooms in the grocery store, keeping the rod within close reach) to spank the child as soon as possible. Spanking soon after the offense also serves our children by relieving them of the apprehension of anticipating the spanking.

Privacy. After about eighteen months, children can be embarrassed by being spanked in front of others. The motive for choosing a private place (bathroom, bedroom, public restroom) is not to hide from others but to protect our children from being humiliated. Sheree and I encourage parents to choose a particular place in the home (not the child's bedroom so he will not associate it with being disciplined), where the spankings are administered routinely.

Neutral Object. Since the Bible speaks of the "rod" of correction, it is always puzzling to us that people find using a paddle offensive. In His wisdom, God directed us away from using our hands—a gentle object of love—as the means of discipline. Using a neutral object also prevents us from stunning our children with a sudden swat that lacks self-control and clarity.

Self-Control. The moments that it takes to get the paddle also give us time to gain control of our emotions. Often, our frustration builds because we have allowed behavior or attitudes that should have been dealt with an hour ago to go unaddressed. Anger, frustration or irritation will not produce healthy fruit in our home. James 1:20 warns us that "man's anger does not bring about the righteous life that God desires."

Identifying and overcoming these areas in our lives will help us see the results we desire in our children.

Restoration. The final aspect of the spanking session is the need for full restoration with the child. Immediately after administering the spanking we should hug the child until he or she finishes crying, affirm our love and acceptance, and have them ask for forgiveness for their disobedience or wrong attitude. In our family, we then add praying for God's forgiveness and help, and have the child thank us for correcting him or her. We have seen this as a valuable and meaningful attitude to develop as our older children are now beginning to learn about appreciating the discipline of God. Last, the child should be restored to anyone he hurt or offended by soliciting that person's forgiveness as well.

Repeating the Situation Properly. The discipline procedure is incomplete without reinforcing the standard by repeating the situation properly. Our intent should be to both discipline and instruct. When a small child disobeys by touching a harmful plant he or she should be disciplined and then brought back to the scene to respond to our command not to touch the plant. When an older child argues disrespectfully with his parent, he should be disciplined and then required to respond politely to the same directive to which he just reacted. This kind of "role play" helps our children learn exactly what we are expecting of them.

To make this procedure as clear as possible, we offer this example with our four-year-old, Janelle.

> Janelle and Joey are playing together. Joey accidentally knocks her blocks down with his elbow.

Janelle: (Pushing him.) *Jooooey!* You knocked my blocks over! (Starts crying.)

Joey: I'm sorry, Missy. It was an accident.

Daddy: (Walks into the room.) What happened, children?

Janelle: Joey knocked my blocks over.

Joey: It was an accident, Daddy. And Missy has something to tell you. [Note: We don't allow tattling among the children.]

Daddy: What do you need to tell me, Missy?

Janelle: Well, when Joey knocked my blocks over, I pushed him.

Daddy: You did? And I also heard you scream at him like this—*Jooooey!* Please come with Daddy to have a spanking.

          (In the bathroom.) Janelle, why does Daddy need to discipline you?

Janelle: Because I screamed at Joey.

Daddy: That's right, and you pushed him, too, right?

Janelle: But he knocked my blocks over, Daddy!

Daddy: Missy, Joey already explained that was an accident. Remember how we've been learning about self-control? Jesus can help you to respond properly when things like that happen. You did not choose to respond properly this time, did you?

Janelle: No, sir.

Daddy: So Daddy must spank you for having a bad attitude toward your brother, right?

Janelle: Right.

(Janelle bends over Daddy's knee and receives her spanking. She cries, Daddy hugs her.)

Daddy: I love you very much, honey. And Jesus and I want to help you to have self-control. Now, what do you need to say?

Janelle: Will you forgive me for having a bad attitude at Joey?

Daddy: Yes, I forgive you. And?

Janelle: And thank you for correcting me.

Daddy: You're welcome, honey. Now you need to ask Jesus to forgive you and help you, O.K.?

Janelle: Jesus, please forgive me for screaming at Joey and pushing him. Help me to have self-control. Amen.

Daddy: Good, honey. Daddy forgives you and Jesus forgives you. Who else needs to forgive you?

Janelle: Joey does.

Daddy: That's right. Now you can ask him to forgive you and we will try this again.

Janelle: (Asks for Joey's forgiveness. They embrace.)

Daddy: Now let's try this over again so you can respond properly, Missy. (Daddy "reconstructs" the scene with the blocks, Joey knocks them over.) Now, how do you respond properly, Missy?

Janelle: (Calmly.) Joey, please try not to knock my blocks down.

Joey: Oh, I'm sorry, Missy. It was an accident. I'll help you put them back.

Janelle: Thanks, Joey.

Daddy: That was tremendous! See how you can choose to have self-control? Thank you for responding so well!

You may be thinking, "You're kidding, aren't you? You actually go through this whole procedure every time you spank your children? Is this all really necessary?"

No, I'm not kidding. Yes, this is our typical procedure, although as our children mature they don't need the reminders and promptings during the process, which shortens it. And, yes, there are times when we selfishly shorten the process because we are in a hurry or want to get back to the newspaper. Other situations don't involve an offense toward another person and, therefore, are not as involved. We feel this commitment to detail is necessary to reinforce our standards and build appreciation for correction.

5. *Why do you discipline for attitudes as well as behavior?* Few parents question the importance of disciplining their children for lying, hurting others or willfully disobeying. Yet some have not heard of spanking for wrong attitudes (being selfish, pouting or whining when a request is denied, or responding with a disrespectful "Why?" to a parent's request).

Remember, our goal is to raise respectful, responsible, responsive children. A child who is allowed to have bad attitudes will retain them as an adult. Certainly the ways in which he expresses selfishness or disrespect will change as he becomes older, but the root will remain intact.

Consider Jesus' death on the cross. Was it only for the murderers and adulterers—those who obviously "needed" to pay for their sins? Certainly not. In fact, Jesus said that those who got angry with their brothers or lusted in their hearts were subject to the same judgment (see Matthew 5:22, 27–28). God's standards include both the outward behavior and the inward attitude of heart. Ours must, too.

6. *Won't spanking my children so regularly strain our relationship and cause them to be afraid of me?*

Remember, using the rod is only a part of the total parent-child relationship. The biggest part of the bond we have with our children comes through playing with, encouraging, praising, building memories and just "hanging out" with them. The emphasis of this chapter might seem to suggest that much of the day is spent in the bathroom spanking the children. (With a large family it can sure feel this way some days!)

Being concerned that your children will be afraid of you is common. Sheree showed me this quote from a 1979 issue of *McCall's* magazine: "Anyone knowledgeable in the field of child psychology knows that physical punishment not only has no beneficial effects for a child, but can be psychologically harmful." "Experts" who take this stance not only lack knowledge themselves but give advice that contradicts God's Word. They need to meet the parents who have seen dramatic and fulfilling results from lovingly and consistently using the rod of correction. You can't argue with success.

Biblical discipline done in the presence of a strong love bond between the parent and child does not produce a fearful child who resents his parents. Rather, it causes the child to become secure in what is expected of him and in the unconditional love and acceptance of his parents. The only fear he has is of wrongdoing—and that will be a healthy contribution to his maturity.

7. *What if this approach just doesn't work with my children?*

This technique of child discipline is not ours alone. With some variance, many people share our philosophies. Because using the rod of correction is a biblical directive, we can have confidence in its effectiveness. Sheree and I know parents who have experienced success in everything from training a two-year-old to stay in bed at night to overcoming disrespectful reactions from a nine-year-old.

Unsuccessful results are not due to the error of the principle. Failure to experience the results are most often linked to one or more of the following: Inconsistency (thus, confusing the child); sinful reactions by parents (disciplining in anger, irritation or frustration); impatience (not allowing an adequate amount of time—which can be many months—for behavior or attitudes to change); weak parental convictions (lacking faith that it will work); or lack of parental peer relationships and example (not exposing ourselves regularly to friends who can model, help, encourage and give us suggestions).

Do you want your children to grow in character, avoiding flaws you still struggle with as an adult? Do you want to help them view hardships from a biblical perspective? Do you long for them to be secure, cooperative and obedient? Would you like to prepare them for their destinies as children of the King of kings? Are you willing to have higher standards than most parents you know?

If your answer to these questions is yes, then God's Word can help you! His methods are tried and timeless. Purpose today to seek Him on this matter. Discuss any changes you desire to make as a couple. Solicit the input of friends who have achieved success. And, if necessary, find a church that emphasizes and instructs parents in successful family living.

Discipline, then, will take on new meaning—for you and your children. Approaching discipline from God's perspective can change our formerly negative thoughts to positive ones: security in our ability to raise our children; confidence in changed attitudes and behavior; increasing maturity; and peace in the home.

Your children will benefit, both now and in the future. Their hunger for God can be the exciting result!

10
Parenting and the Grace of God

Sheree

Several years ago we were in a church in another city giving our "Parenting: From Survival to Success" seminar. On the following Sunday morning we attended the Sunday meeting of the sponsoring church. Afterward, I made my way toward the children's classrooms.

As I left the main meeting room I heard what I thought was a familiar sound: Jesse crying (or should I say shouting?).

Sure enough, when I entered the lobby area of the building I encountered a terrible scene. Joshua had taken the initiative to gather the children from their classes, thinking this would help Benny and me. He had no idea, unfortunately, that three-year-old Jesse would protest having to leave the classroom. Joshua tried patiently to take his hand so he could take him to one of us. As I came onto the scene, Jesse had begun to cry and scream, *"Leave me alone!"* at the top of his lungs.

A small crowd of people had gathered, watching Jesse's temper escalate. Finally, he fell to the floor and sobbed, "Where's Mommy? Leave me alone and find Mommy!"

I must admit I had fleeting thoughts of slipping quietly out the door, past those who were wondering whose screaming child this was.

The look of relief on poor Joshua's face when he saw me walking toward them brought me back to reality. "Here's Mommy, Jesse," he said as all eyes in the room turned toward me.

"Jesse," I said as I reached to pick him up, "stop screaming. Mommy's here. Come on, honey." I could feel the awkwardness and concern of those who were watching. By this time he was well into a temper tantrum, continuing to protest having to leave the children's ministry. He was unaffected by my presence and continued to cry and tried to get away from me.

As I carried my screaming child into the restroom close by, I had to chuckle at God's sense of humor: Here was a child of the couple who came to town to help other people train *their* children, putting on quite a display! I spent quite some time calming Jesse down, disciplining him for his wrong attitude, re-disciplining for refusing to receive his spanking willingly, and completing the restoration process. When I noticed an expectant mother leaving the restroom, I hoped she was still happy about having a baby who would someday become a three-year-old!

Situations like this can tempt even the most committed parent to give up. After several years of consistent training, we were still dealing with behavior and attitudes in our son that many totally undisciplined children don't exhibit! Yes, Benny and I are not exempt from difficult challenges with our children. They were born with as much foolishness in their hearts as anyone else's. This recognition has protected us from resenting their imperfections and has helped us to focus on the important issue of how to motivate them to *want* to become responsive.

Maybe you aren't trying to help a child overcome temper tantrums. Perhaps you simply want to train your son to sit politely in his chair and eat his food or teach your daughter to keep her bedroom tidy. Whatever your goal, motivating them is essential to lasting success.

I would say, in fact, that motivating our children to want to mature is perhaps the most crucial part of their training. And to accomplish this we must first evaluate our own motives.

Our goal, for instance, in helping Jesse overcome his immature, angry reactions was not simply to avoid embarrassing situations like the one above (although I must admit this was a factor!). He may have grown out of such childish tantrums in a few years, but his anger and resistance to our authority would have been manifested in other ways. Any plumber can tell you that plugging one hole in a defective pipe will do little to stop the leaking. The water will simply spring out from the holes that have not been repaired.

Do we want to train our children to keep their rooms neat because we are personally irritated by messiness? Or do we see the long-range importance of building responsibility and diligence into their character? Is our commitment to requiring respectful responses primarily because we refuse to have "smart-mouthed" children? Or do we hope to build a strong foundation of self-control, humility and respect for authority into their lives?

Asking ourselves these difficult questions will help us discern why we do what we do. As we allow God to work proper motives into our own hearts, we will be more able to impart values to them.

Benny and I feel that the most important key to imparting our values, rather than simply requiring adherence to them, is to motivate our children in grace. Because of the importance of this issue I will discuss it for the remainder of this chapter.

Motivating by Grace

Some years ago, I would not have responded to Jesse's public display as I did. I would have been extremely embarrassed. In the privacy of the restroom I might have reacted harshly and angrily toward Jesse. I would have felt very self-conscious around those who had witnessed the "scene" or might have blamed Joshua for not waiting for me to get him from the children's ministry. Being able to see the situation from God's perspective—a strong-willed three-year-old throwing a temper tantrum and a parent with an opportunity to have humility worked into her life—was possible only because of an understanding of God's grace.

God was not "embarrassed" by Jesse's behavior. Neither was He angry or frustrated. He probably viewed it as another indication of a child's need to overcome anger and selfishness. This should be my perspective as well.

Our relationship with our Father is not based on how we perform for Him. His grace—His unmerited favor and acceptance—is extended to His children despite our failings, weaknesses and sin. God's unconditional love was proven two thousand years ago in that "while we were still sinners, Christ died for us" (Romans 5:8). He loves us no more or less today than on that day when His blood was shed on our behalf while we were in a rotten, sinful state.

Our salvation has nothing to do with us and everything to do with Him. Suggesting that God's acceptance is based on our performance is the legalistic sin of the Pharisees that Jesus condemned.

Am I suggesting that we simply accept our children's failings and sinfulness? No, of course not. I am, however, attempting to underscore the importance of seeing that all of their teaching, disciplining and correcting be done in grace.

They must feel our unconditional love. They must be assured that no matter how many times they disobey, we will always love and accept them—even when we cannot accept their wrong behavior or attitudes.

Peter asked Jesus once how many times he should forgive someone. Seven times? Jesus answered, seventy times seven, meaning that we should be willing to persevere long past when it seems "reasonable" to us (Matthew 18:21–22). The same applies to training our children. We must persevere as long as it takes.

Paul offers another helpful insight on this matter in Romans 3:20: "Therefore, no one will be declared righteous in his sight by observing the law; rather, through the law we become conscious of sin." Our children should not feel that adherence to our "code of conduct" in the home is the way to merit our love and acceptance—just as merely obeying the law does not gain us favor with God. Our love, like the love of God, must be unconditional. It should not be based on whether or not they obey, but on the fact that they are our children.

Such an atmosphere helps our children want to obey because they don't fear our rejection if they disobey.

Many children react negatively to high standards because they feel that no amount of effort on their part can achieve them. Most children like to have a tidy bedroom, for example, but they can feel frustrated when their efforts to clean it get responses like: "But you forgot to do this and you didn't put that away." They feel as if their efforts are unappreciated and never good enough to warrant Mom or Dad's approval.

You may be thinking, "If my son simply put a *little* effort into his room I'd be happy. No, I don't appreciate his efforts because he barely does enough to keep it from being condemned by the health department! If I want it to get done, I have to do it."

Benny and I are not suggesting that you be content with

halfhearted, lazy efforts. That is a separate issue. It shows an irresponsible child who must be trained systematically to be responsible, as we discussed in chapter seven.

The issue here is not their training but our attitude toward them. Is our interaction, communication and response characterized by acceptance of them regardless of their performance?

My friend Jean is the mother of five. She and her husband, Mike, were recently preparing the children for a large family reunion. Jean was especially interested in using the opportunity to remind her six-year-old daughter, Rachel, of her need to be gracious, warm and polite when interacting with relatives they saw infrequently.

After they returned home from the outing Jean took the opportunity to encourage Rachel.

"Rachel, I noticed how well you were talking with everyone today," she began. "I noticed how you thanked someone politely for saying your dress was pretty, and I appreciated how you used people's names when you greeted them."

Smiling, Rachel responded, "O.K. But?" She obviously assumed that Jean would follow her encouragement with some ways in which she could have done better.

Jean was surprised. In fact, she did have something she wanted to mention to Rachel that was corrective in nature, but knew this was not the time.

"No 'buts,' honey. I'm very pleased with how well you did today."

"Thanks, Mom," Rachel replied, giving Jean a big hug and kiss.

This situation caused Jean and Mike to realize the need for change in relating to Rachel. At only six years of age, Rachel was noticing how often her parents preceded admonishment with encouragement. They did not want their daughter to view affirmation as a primer for correction. Neither did they want Rachel to grow up feeling that she could never perform well enough—no matter how hard she tried—to earn Mom and Dad's sincere encouragement. Mike and Jean recognized this tendency as a subtle form of legalism in their parenting skills.

When we became parents some thirteen years ago, Benny and I did not understand this concept of grace in parenting. Only in beginning to understand the grace of God toward us, His children, did we begin to make some changes in our responses to our children.

In the early years of parenting we were, like most new parents, eager to do a good job with the children we were given. Medical complications had suggested that we would not have children. When Joshua came after three years of trying to conceive, we were deeply grateful to God for this gift and we desired to raise him with godly standards. We soon discovered that we lacked grace in implementing the standards.

When Josh was just over two years old, we left him with Nannie for the weekend. While we were away we missed him terribly. We had taken one-year-old Jaime with us and were enjoying the time alone with her, but we missed our little guy a lot.

On the way home we talked about being able to see him. Maybe we could take him out for some ice cream after dinner. We couldn't wait to see the look on his face when Mommy and Daddy walked into the house! We were sure he had missed us almost as much as we had missed him.

We walked quietly up to Nannie's front door, hoping to surprise him. We opened the door gently, peering in to see if he was within view. Great! He was sitting at the dining room table with Nannie. This was going to be fun.

"Hi, Joshua!" we yelled as we swung open the door.

"Hi," he said casually, taking another bite of Nannie's homemade chocolate cake. (So much for an ice cream outing together.)

"Honey, come and greet Mommy and Daddy and Jaime," Benny said. "We've been gone for three days and we missed you."

"Can I finish my cake first?" he asked.

Our hearts dropped. We had received better greetings after running a twenty-minute errand to the hardware store! In our immaturity we overreacted. We took this opportunity to remind Joshua of the importance of greeting others warmly, something we had been working on for some time.

"Josh, please get down and come and greet us," I said.

Making this an issue invoked a wrong response from him. "But I want to finish my cake first," he whined.

"Honey, you may not whine and have a bad attitude," Benny warned. "Obey Daddy and greet us properly, please."

One thing led to the next and soon Joshua was in the bathroom being disciplined for his attitudes. Our expectations of a warm and happy homecoming and a fun evening together were ruined.

Was it wrong to correct Joshua for his improper greeting? No, because for months we had been helping him develop polite greeting habits. He was well aware of the way in which he should welcome others. Was it immature to take it personally when our two-year-old, who had little concept of how long we had been gone, didn't leave his chocolate cake and run to greet us? Yes. Our expectations caused us to react (not respond) to him and use the wrong situation as a "learning opportunity." Basically, we were disappointed that he wasn't as glad to see us as we were him. We communicated this disappointment through a legalistic enforcement of our greeting standard.

How might we handle this situation with little son Jacob today? We would still be as eager to see him. We might still hope to take him out for ice cream. And we might sneak up to the house to surprise him, but upon finding him at the table eating Nannie's chocolate cake, we would probably greet him and then ask for a piece of cake ourselves! We would choose other times to train him in proper greeting skills.

You may think it odd that we made an issue of Joshua's disappointing greeting. Yes, we were foolish. But, before you think too badly of us, consider that everyone at some time or other has handled a situation in a similarly selfish or immature way. Maybe it involved the care of their belongings, a fight with a sibling or disobedience over completing a household task. Has your quickness to address a problem always been based on a desire to train and instruct? Or sometimes was it because you were disappointed or angry?

All of us parents misrepresent God to our children when we lack grace in the way we relate to them. Right or wrong, we influence heavily their concept of God and His attributes. As the years pass, they begin to associate our view of them with God's view of them, our love of them with God's love of them, our rejection of them with God's rejection of them.

What is evidence of a lack of grace in your relationship with your children?

Symptoms	*Suggested Solutions*
Focusing inordinately on their weaknesses by minimizing their development, growth and strengths.	Look for the positive and encourage, affirm and reward them.

Symptoms	*Suggested Solutions*
Using threats and other manipulative ways to get them to respond ("After all I do for you, can't you do this one thing for me?" or "You'd better obey or I'm going to call Daddy").	Recognize this tendency and ask for help from others (spouse, close friend) to overcome it. Pray regularly for God's help in this area.
Fulfilling your parental responsibilities mechanically and without faith.	Search your heart for resentment/bitterness. Begin to think of your responsibilities in a positive way. Spend some extra time having fun with the children.
Consistently lacking joy in parenthood.	Identify any areas of self-sufficiency, bitterness, fear, laziness in your life. Seek out relationships with parents who obviously enjoy their children.
Showing favoritism to one child over another because of his/her level of obedience or responsiveness (giving more affection, expressions of love, time).	Repent of wrong attitudes toward the less responsive child. Spend time with him/her. Look for ways to affirm and show your love.
Using anger, harshness or obvious irritation to force obedience (leads to child feeling rejected when he disobeys, accepted when he obeys).	Develop an alternative plan for relating to your children (kindness, patience). Meditate on Scriptures. Communicate regularly your love, acceptance—"I like *and* love you"—and repent of any sin that will prohibit change in this area.

Symptoms	*Suggested Solutions*
Frequent feelings of failure as a parent *not* based on real conviction over sinful attitudes toward the children.	Consider factors in your relationship to God and your upbringing that may cause these feelings. Resist any condemning thoughts that you aren't "cut out" for parenting.
Weariness of heart (frequently feeling you can't fulfill your responsibilities, "this is too hard," etc.).	Evaluate your relationship with God. Are you growing spiritually? Do you rely on Him for the strength you need as a parent?
Regular inconsistency— "looking the other way"—when areas need to be addressed and dealt with in the children. Noticing your children obeying when you're around but disobeying when you're not.	Identify areas of personal lack that cause this response (laziness, resenting being inconvenienced by them, selfishness). Consider your need to affirm and show acceptance to them more regularly.

If several of the above symptoms apply to you, then a lack of grace in relating to your children is something you will want to consider. Discuss this with your spouse and a few close friends.

Don't be discouraged! God can change you! The changes won't come because you "try harder." Rather, they will come as you study God's Word, allow His Spirit to convict you (that is, convince you of the wrongness of sin), and cooperate with those changes He initiates in your life.

Several years ago one of our children went through a bout with lying. Over a several-month period Benny and I discovered a number of occasions of deception to avoid being caught doing something wrong. Yet each time God saw that we were made aware of the incident.

After this child was disciplined for the third time for the same offense, discouragement in our child set in: "Why do I keep doing this when I know it's wrong? I keep thinking I won't lie again and then I do. What's wrong with me?"

We, too, were somewhat discouraged. We were puzzled over why our usually honest, eager-to-please child was suddenly dealing with lying. Yet we understood the temptation. We, too, have dealt with the frustration of thinking we should be "further along" than our weaknesses and recurring sins indicated.

Was God, our Father, discouraged and frustrated with us? No. Was He pacing angrily, wringing His hands and wondering if we would ever change? No. Was He willing to accept our weaknesses as "just the way we were"? No.

Good. Then once again the Father's model provided what we needed in our response to our child.

"We understand how frustrated you are. We know that deep in your heart you don't *want* to lie. You feel bad when you're dishonest, right?"

"Yes, I do. I keep wondering when you'll find out."

"Jesus loves you so much that He allows us to find out so we can help you to change, honey. Besides, it doesn't matter how many times you disobey, we will always love you. It hurts us when you are dishonest, but it doesn't affect how very much we love you. We will always discipline you when you disobey, but even that's because of how much we love you and want to help you to change. Do you understand, honey?"

Even as we were talking, Benny and I realized that only a revelation of God's grace equipped us to respond to our child this way. Everything in our natural thinking wanted to pour on enough guilt to ensure we were never lied to again. In the past we surely had given into such a temptation—assuming that raising our voices, frowning hard enough or lecturing long enough would produce the desired results.

How unlike the Father we are! He doesn't condone our sin. In fact, He insists that we walk in holiness before Him, producing fruit that is proof of genuine repentance (Matthew 3:8). Yet He provides the way through grace so we don't lose heart. Just as His grace doesn't lower His criteria for holiness, our grace won't cause us to lower our standards in the home.

You may wonder if it is wrong for children to obey and perform simply to please their parents. Could this be an indication of legalism—performing to gain acceptance and love? Not always. All young children obey to avoid the consequences and to please Mommy and Daddy. As they grow into the elementary and pre-adolescent years, however, they should feel more and more secure in our total love, acceptance and availability. This alone will guard them from the fear of rejection.

An accurate picture of God's grace doesn't cause us to take advantage of His forgiveness and acceptance. Rather, it motivates us to walk in holiness all the more (Romans 6:14)! That is what motivating our children by grace should do also.

Titus 2:11–14 gives us some helpful insight on grace and obedience:

> For the grace of God that brings salvation has appeared to all men. It teaches us to say "No" to ungodliness and worldly passions, and to live self-controlled, upright and godly lives in this present age, while we wait for the blessed hope—the glorious appearing of our great God

and Savior, Jesus Christ, who gave himself for us to
redeem us from all wickedness and to purify for himself
a people that are his very own, *eager to do what is
good.*

What an exciting promise! Learning to relate to our children in grace can produce exactly what we are looking for—
the motivation (eagerness) to "do what is good."

This kind of lifestyle, one that is "self-controlled, upright
and godly," will not happen in their lives by our nagging,
manipulating, shouting. Their success will come best by our
modeling the way in which God, our Father, motivates us
with His unconditional and unmerited love.

Do you need to seek God on this matter of grace? Consider
prayerfully the symptoms of lack of grace (legalism) on
pages 153–155. Repent of any wrong ways in which you have
been relating to your children. Be patient with the time it
takes these changes to unfold in your life. Like us, you may
find that some misunderstanding about grace has hampered
both your home life and your relationship with God.

Correcting it will better equip you to motivate your children to be "eager to do what is good."

11
Keys to Motivating Children Successfully

Sheree

You may be beginning to feel somewhat overwhelmed at some of the changes needed in your home. Maybe you are feeling as though you have had low standards for your children's behavior. Maybe you have older children who have not been trained to be respectful, responsible and responsive and you are wondering if you'll be able to recover the lost ground. Or maybe you are realizing that you have lacked grace in the way you've been relating to them.

Welcome to the club! Many Christian parents feel the same. We seem to try our best and are left confused and discouraged when our children don't develop the way we had hoped and prayed for.

Maybe you are experiencing these frustrated feelings over

a toddler who throws tantrums at Grandmother's, a school-aged child who is a discipline problem for the teacher, or an adolescent whose relationship with the Lord is fading. Challenges like these usually produce one of two parental reactions. Either we give in to bitterness—blaming God, withdrawing from the child, lowering our standards to keep peace rather than investing the hard work to see the situation through in faith—or we "pull ourselves up by the bootstraps" and try to force them to change. Meanwhile, we minimize our need for the help and input of others, or we make promise after promise to do better.

We can do better and motivation is the key.

We have already discussed the most crucial element in motivating our children: grace. We can now undergird this foundation with some practical supports.

Motivating with Affection

Many parents find it easy and natural to show affection to their children, especially in the early years. To others it is almost awkward. Our ability to show affection often relates to our upbringing. That is, those who come from warmly affectionate homes tend to be expressive toward their children.

As noted earlier, like it or not, we tend to duplicate our upbringing in our relationships with our children.

Why is affection so important?

First, affection communicates our availability and acceptance tangibly. Hugging, touching, kissing and holding our children meet their needs for visible expressions of our love. They often interpret affection as a form of encouragement or reward, and respond to it by wanting to please us.

Second, affection provides a proper role model. Year after

year, our affectionate overtures train them to be warmly responsive to others. In later years, especially when they have their own children, they will have had an effective example to follow.

Third, affection helps establish security and stability in the home. Children benefit from seeing their parents holding hands or hugging at the kitchen sink. They enjoy being patted spontaneously by Mommy or wrestling with Daddy on the floor.

Few parents fail to give their very young children lots of affection, but many parents neglect it with their older children.

This may be because some children seem to resist affection as they age. They may stiffen when hugged or appear embarrassed when kissed goodnight, things they willingly cooperated with only months before. Wise parents will not take this personally. Rather, they will continue to show affection, realizing it is a need children have of which they are unaware.

My nephew Doug stands at six feet two inches tall and weighs 220 pounds. During his early teenage years he experienced this somewhat typical phase of awkwardness with displays of affection. He didn't blatantly resist us, but his discomfort was clear. He was growing . . . and growing . . . and seemed to feel that the days of playful affection were a little childish. After all, how many young men his size still hugged and kissed their family goodbye?

We honored his request to refrain from calling him a certain pet name (I promised we wouldn't put it in print!) but didn't back off on the affection—something that is a natural quality in my extended family. Over time, as with most teenagers, he came out of his self-consciousness and became his formerly responsive self. When he left recently for boot camp in the Navy, he was warmly and expressively responsive to all our displays of affection.

You may not feel comfortable showing affection to your children—especially your sons. I am not suggesting that you forcibly imitate the kinds of overtures we've mentioned. Rather, I recommend that you see affection as an excellent way to provide the kind of atmosphere in the home that will motivate your children to return your love by showing you their respect.

Motivating with Rewards

We have already discussed the value of rewarding our children in chapter seven. Our discussion at this point will focus on the way well-chosen rewards can contribute to the process of motivating our children.

Have you ever received a special financial bonus or citation for excellence on the job? Maybe you worked especially hard on a particular project or invested extra hours. Receiving a meaningful reward for your service probably made you feel appreciated and valued. You enjoyed the sense of fulfillment and probably were inclined to do it again if called on.

Our children, likewise, benefit from rewards. They help them want to repeat the behavior. Here are two ways to make rewards meaningful in your relationship with your children.

1. Reward character, not performance.

Rewards are a biblical reality (see 2 Timothy 4:8; Luke 6:23; Hebrews 10:35). And, as we have mentioned, it is important to acknowledge character over performance. This prevents our children from learning to do well only to receive a reward and affirms what is most important to God—their inward maturity, not merely their outward performance. In 1 Corinthians 3 we read that Paul was addressing those in the church who were overemphasizing their allegiance to certain men. This was causing division and jealousy in the church. He offered this important point in verses 6–8:

> I planted the seed [of the Gospel]; Apollos watered it, but God made it grow. So neither he who plants nor he who waters is anything, but only God, who makes things grow. The man who plants and the man who waters have one purpose, and *each will be rewarded according to his own labor.*

Notice that the reward from God was not for what either man accomplished. Rather, it was for their unselfish labor. Rewards should focus on their character: diligence, unselfishness, perseverance or extra effort to complete a certain task.

2. Exercise discernment.

We don't want our children to expect to be rewarded at every turn. ("Mommy, I picked up my toys so can I have a cookie?") We should choose the timing and reasons carefully. Rewards should be given for consistent superb behavior; extraordinary deeds of service to others; visible progress in overcoming wrong attitudes; or selfless expressions of love.

Here are some ways Benny and I have rewarded our children that may help to stimulate your thoughts in this area:

- Taking Jaime out for a milkshake to thank her for accompanying us on a trip to care for Jacob. We affirmed her cheerful *servanthood, sweet attitudes* toward Jacob, and desire to bless us by *not complaining*

about the amount of time she had to spend alone with
him.

- Giving Jesse $5.00 to spend at a toy store for filling up
  his "self-control" chart on the refrigerator. We
  thanked him for *working so hard* to overcome his
  wrong reactions when others won the game he was
  playing or when a sibling instead of him was asked to
  accompany Mom or Dad. We especially commended
  him for his *perseverance* to accumulate thirty marks,
  which took nearly a month to do!
- Purchasing a pretty pink toothbrush set for Janelle for
  her *obedience* in overcoming the habit of saying *No!*
  to her siblings. We thanked her for *working so hard* to
  remember to say "No, thank you" instead.

Motivating with Verbal Affirmation and Encouragement

As parents, we have the staggering responsibility of determining how our children feel about themselves. *Am I a
success or a failure? Am I ugly or attractive? Am I enjoyable
or a nuisance? Am I smart or dumb?* The greatest hindrance
to a healthy sense of self-worth is feeling unaccepted.

Encouragement is an outstanding motivational tool to protect them from such self-doubt. With it we can give them the
determination to excel in their areas of strength and mature
in their areas of weakness. Proverbs says, "The tongue has
the power of life and death," and, "Pleasant words are a
honeycomb, sweet to the soul and healing to the bones"
(18:21; 16:24). Our words can build our children up or tear
them down. What a responsibility!

The Bible instructs us to "encourage one another daily"
(Hebrews 3:13) and to "encourage the timid" (1 Thessalonians 5:14). Paul exhorts us to dwell on those things that are

true, noble, right, pure, lovely, admirable, excellent or praiseworthy in others (Philippians 4:8).

Why is encouragement so effective? Because every person longs for the approval of others.

Benny and I gauge the need for extra encouragement on the following responses in our children:

- Apathy—A general feeling of disinterest in responsibilities or relationships (indifference, unresponsiveness, lethargy).
- Fear—Unwillingness to try new things; inordinate concern about failing or embarrassing themselves. Often anxious or apprehensive, especially in situations in which they lack confidence.
- "I can't" mentality—Assuming incompetence even before they have made an attempt.
- Being overly assertive—Often trying to prove themselves in situations in which they are insecure or feel awkward.
- Resistance—Refusing to involve themselves in situations or relationships because they may fail or they lack the skills to feel confident.
- Excessive shyness—Inordinate inability to relate to people; no eye contact; avoidance of social situations; "loner" mentality.
- Irresponsibility—Lack of growth in assuming responsibilities in the home.

Encouragement is helping many children we have contact with to overcome such things as these. Simple affirmation like "You're so helpful!" "What a responsible little girl you're becoming!" "Thank you for working so hard to clean the bathroom" and "You're such a gift from God to me!" help to ensure that our children *feel* our love and will motivate them to mature all the more.

In areas of weakness or lack in a particular child, visualize the child the way you desire him or her to be and then encourage any movement in that direction. By faith, picture your stubborn child as cooperative and then thank him for even the little ways in which he is cooperative. Envision the one who seems to enjoy his messy room as a neat and well-organized child and then affirm any ways in which he shows an interest in order. A lifestyle of encouragement begins with looking for the positive.

Motivating with Role Play

Young children learn best when instruction is reinforced in multiple ways. They may learn to tie their shoes, for example, simply by watching their parents do so year after year. They will learn more quickly, however, by watching (using visual skills), being "talked through" the process (using audio skills), and then trying it themselves (using motor skills).

Role play—actually acting out our standards for them—helps children understand what is expected of them. Let's say your four-year-old rolls her eyes and makes a face when she's told it is time for bed.

One approach would be to say something like, "Honey, please don't react like that when I tell you it's time for bed. That is a wrong attitude. Remember, Mommy wants you to respond cheerfully and willingly, O.K.?"

React like what? your daughter could be thinking. *I didn't do anything. What is wrong with my attitude?*

A four-year-old couldn't articulate her thought in this way. Yet the confusion would exist all the same. Addressing her wrong attitude is good, and after many times of correcting her she may catch on to what you expect of her.

A more effective way would be this. You give her a five-minute warning that it will soon be time for bed. This helps minimize being surprised and can offset wrong reactions. Five minutes later the scenario may happen something like this:

Dad:	O.K., honey, it's bedtime. Let's go and brush your teeth and get into bed.
Daughter:	[Doesn't respond verbally but sighs, rolls her eyes, is obviously unhappy.]
Dad:	Honey, look at Daddy. That is an unacceptable way to respond when I tell you it is bedtime. Here, you come and be the daddy and I'll be the little girl. [Dad gets on the floor, daughter on the couch. Make sure you have her full attention.] Now, you say, "Honey, it's time for bed."
Daughter:	Honey, it's time for bed.
Dad:	[Duplicates daughter's sour facial expressions and sighing.] See, honey, that's how you responded. Now, let's try it again and I will show you how to respond properly.
Daughter:	Honey, it's time for bed.
Dad:	[Cheerfully] O.K., Daddy! [Stands up and starts toward the bathroom.] See? That's how Daddy wants you to respond. Now let's try it all over again. [Dad and daughter switch back to original places and rehearse the situation again.]

Role play is most helpful for young children, but parents of teenagers have even seen results with an adaptation of situations like that above.

You may be wondering what you would do if your daughter doesn't respond properly after your demonstration. If you are sure she understood what was expected and yet she did not repeat the situation properly you would address her disobedience and discipline with the rod. After disciplining her, you should take her back to the same spot and repeat the instruction to go to bed. If she responds properly you can praise her. If not, you can repeat the discipline and try again until she responds properly. Enforcing this every night at bedtime will produce changed attitudes.

Role play is effective for many reasons. It makes a clear presentation of our standards. It forces us to think through exactly what we are expecting of our children. It removes the misunderstandings and confusion of adult vocabulary. It injects lightheartedness into potentially difficult circumstances (children love seeing Mom and Dad act as they do!). It gives us the opportunity to model appropriate behavior and attitudes. And, most important, it ensures us that our children understand our directives.

What are some areas in which role play is most helpful?

- Demonstrating voice tones (helping them to overcome "baby voice," whining, disrespectful responses, harshness with siblings, lack of cheerfulness).
- Correcting improper facial expressions (frowning, scowling, refusing eye contact, hiding behind parents, rolling their eyes).
- Addressing improper responses to conflict (argumentativeness, selfishness with their belongings, unwillingness to ask forgiveness).
- Demonstrating standards in areas of responsibility (neatness, thoroughness, attitudes when asked to serve in the home).

Role play is easier for us when we, as parents, understand the importance of clarity in communicating our standards to our children. We must not feel self-conscious about looking juvenile or silly because we are on the floor acting out our toddler's temper tantrum or flopping angrily onto the sofa as our older child just did. Our children will appreciate the lengths to which we are willing to go.

Motivating with Correction

We have already discussed the importance of consistent, loving discipline in training respectful, responsive and responsible children. Our emphasis at this point concerns the motivational aspects of child discipline.

It is easy to see how grace, affection, rewards, encouragement and role play could be effective motivational tools for our children. But discipline? How can discipline do anything but simply deter them from disobeying and displaying wrong attitudes? How can correction be a positive, motivating factor in their lives?

Once again, we must resist the tendency to view correction as "negative." Yes, it is unpleasant and painful, but the fruit that it produces suggests that it is a positive, helpful, valuable part of life. When done consistently and lovingly, correction can be as effective as the more pleasant ways to motivate children that we have discussed thus far.

How, specifically, does discipline provide incentive for our children to excel in behavior and attitudes?

First, it cultivates in them respect for authority. This attitude does not characterize today's generation of young people. This is often because those in positions of authority have not exercised a proper amount of discipline.

Dr. T. Berry Brazelton was asked in *U.S. News & World*

Report if today's parents are exercising more discipline in the home than our counterparts in previous decades:

> In the '50s and '60s parents were afraid of being disciplinarians. That left the kids high and dry. Now I think we have come to the realization that a parent's role is really to show youngsters discipline. That means parents have to think about such questions as "What do I value?" At the point the child gets provocative and the parent knows he or she is looking for a limit, the parent better provide it. And the child will be reassured for having limits set. Children need limits spelled out for them. It is the only way they learn.

Children who do not respect authority are in danger of severe consequences. Romans 13:2 warns us that "he who rebels against the authority is rebelling against what God has instituted, and those who do so will bring judgment on themselves." Discipline—both in the form of spanking and a general enforcement of rules and standards in the home—helps our children to avoid such judgment.

Second, discipline helps our children to obey. Although many children choose to receive repeated spankings for their misbehavior, eventually they wise up to the fact that Mom and Dad aren't going to give up on this. They learn what is expected, feel more secure and ultimately feel protected and loved. What better motivation to cooperate with our rules and standards than to avoid the consequences!

Third, loving correction develops godly character. Children are born with a bent toward sin that draws them toward selfishness, disobedience and rebellion. Some children display these tendencies more outwardly than others, yet apart from God's saving grace we are all in bondage to sinful habits and desires.

First Corinthians 13:11 says, "When I was a child, I talked like a child, I thought like a child, I reasoned like a child. When I became a man, I put childish ways behind me." It is naïve to think that this process will happen instantly on a child's eighteenth birthday! Doing away with childish things is a process that begins early and progresses steadily. Discipline is an important part of the maturing process.

Fourth, discipline helps our children discover their spiritual gifts and callings. As well-trained children grow older, their gifts and talents begin to emerge. They begin to feel certain stirrings of how God may want to use them to serve Him and others. The thrilling result is that they become spiritually ambitious and courageous. We will discuss more about this exciting area later.

Last, discipline causes our children to appreciate and learn from reproof. Children who are allowed to resist their parents' correction typically become arrogant and self-sufficient (see Proverbs 12:1; 26:12).

Several years ago, when Josh was nine, we noticed his tendency to be overly competitive. We appreciated his aggressiveness and courage, but wanted to help him overcome having to be "right" about everything, such as whether or not someone was "safe" at first base. Basically, we wanted him to learn to be humble and flexible when he played with others. We suggested that he mention this to some close friends and ask for their help.

When his friend Andy came over the following week he pulled him aside before they started a football game.

"Andy," he said, "my parents have been talking to me about how I have prideful attitudes sometimes when I'm playing games. You know, how I argue about things that aren't that important and want everyone to let me decide the rules? Well, I wondered if you would point these things out if I do them while we're playing."

This was the beginning of Josh's commitment to overcoming overly competitive attitudes in sports without losing his intensity and aggressiveness. The next year he and Andy were on a basketball team together and he asked for both Andy's and the coach's help in this area.

At thirteen, Josh still struggles with symptoms of being overly competitive. He is still growning in self-control and humility . . . and he still loves being "right." His personality suggests that this temptation will always be present, but he is learning to value the input and correction of others in overcoming character weaknesses that would hamper his maturity.

We've learned a lot from his response!

Motivating By Our Example

About now you may be thinking, "Whew! How in the world do you remember to do all of this encouraging, rewarding, showing affection and disciplining? Benny, how do you have time to pastor a church? And Sheree, how can you keep up with a home and six children?"

It can feel overwhelming! It helps to remember, though, that the goal is not simply to do better at parenting. Understanding the grace of God helps all of us parents approach changes in our home from a less stressful perspective. It releases us from the pressure to perform better and helps us make systematic changes in response to God's conviction and direction.

His faithfulness is new every morning. This means you can start tomorrow to be more encouraging and affectionate. You can explain to your children that they will now be disciplined for disobedience and wrong attitudes that have gone unaddressed.

Many parents attempt to help their children to mature by saying, "This is the way I want you to go, now go for it." Then they get behind them—prodding, pushing and correcting—hoping that their efforts will help their children move toward their goals for them. In many cases, the progress is painfully slow, and Mom and Dad end up tired and discouraged.

Wise parents choose another method of motivating their children. Rather than get behind them, they *reach for* them and, from a position of strength, gently lead them. Such parents are pace-setters who recognize the importance of both declaring *and* demonstrating their goals for their children.

And these parents find that all of the ways in which we motivate our children help to cultivate their hearts for God. How? By helping them want to know the God of grace who will love, reward, encourage and—yes—discipline them.

This won't be accomplished by simply implementing new ways of relating to them. It can be done best by provoking them to godly jealousy by the lifestyle we live. Our relationship with Jesus Christ can help us better understand His grace and to become more affirming, encouraging and consistent in our discipline. But most importantly, our visible thirst for God—expressed in how we seek to conform to the image of His Son—can cause a similar desire in them to know and serve Jesus Christ.

12
A Mother's Influence

Sheree

When Winston Churchill was asked to approve a list given to him of those teachers who had most influenced his life, he returned the list with this response: "You have failed to mention the greatest of my teachers—my mother."

Abraham Lincoln said, "All that I am and all that I shall be, I owe to my mother."

We mothers have a rare privilege: A mother can have an influence on her children that no one else can. We also have a great responsibility: to see that our influence builds upon our children for good. Consider these biblical examples.

- Jochebed—Moses' mother who risked her life to save her son from being killed (Exodus 2:1–3).
- Hannah—Samuel's mother who, after waiting for years to have a child, willingly gave him to the Lord for service (1 Samuel 1:21–22).
- Mary—The mother of Jesus who helped Him grow "in wisdom and in stature, and in favor with God and men" (Luke 2:51–52).

- Elizabeth—John the Baptist's mother who helped him become "strong in spirit" (Luke 1:80).
- Eunice—Timothy's mother, of whom Paul said: "I have been reminded of your sincere faith, which first lived in your grandmother Lois and in your mother Eunice and, I am persuaded, now lives in you also" (2 Timothy 1:5).

Now look at those whose sway was negative. Rebecca led her son Jacob to deceive his dying father in order to obtain Esau's blessing (Genesis 27:5–10). Herodias counseled her daughter to request that John the Baptist be beheaded (Matthew 14:6–8). The harmful influence of those mothers had severe consequences in others' lives.

How can we maximize our positive influence as mothers? We must first understand the importance of our role in our children's lives.

A Mother's Worth

Our society often devalues the role of mothers because it does not understand the place a woman holds for her children. A mother is much more than the biological source vehicle from which life comes. She is the primary source of nurturing, caring, comforting, training, guiding and instructing for her children. We can find great fulfillment in this God-given privilege. Sure, any healthy woman can give birth, change diapers and wash baby clothes, but not "just anyone" can raise children into mature, responsible adulthood.

What are some biblical examples of a proper perspective on our role as mothers? Below are some characteristics the Bible attributes to mothers:

- Gentleness—"We were gentle among you, like a mother caring for her little children" (1 Thessalonians 2:7).
- Joy and happiness—"He settles the barren woman in her home as a happy mother of children" (Psalm 113:9).
- Hope—"Discipline your son, for in that there is hope" (Proverbs 19:18).
- Gratitude—"May your father and mother be glad; may she who gave you birth rejoice!" (Proverbs 23:25).
- Peace and delight—"Discipline your son, and he will give you peace; he will bring delight to your soul" (Proverbs 29:17).

Am I suggesting that only the mother who exhibits these qualities consistently is a good mother? Certainly not. We have too many character weaknesses to display this fruit in our lives every day! (Like yesterday, when Jesse spilled a pitcher of sweetened iced tea on my newly waxed kitchen floor!)

Our goal isn't perfection, but progression. Ask yourself, "Am I growing in gentleness, joy, gratitude, peace and hope in my relationship with my children?" If not, you might first look for areas of unconfessed sin (resentment, anger, unbelief, impatience). You can then more properly evaluate your influence as a mother.

Common Obstacles to Effective Motherhood

As mothers, we have certain hopes for our relationships with our children. We want to enjoy a strong bond of love and trust. We long for them to become responsible and spiritually passionate. We want our influence in their lives to be positive and inspiring. Yet we all encounter certain obstacles to these desires.

The first obstacle to effective motherhood is not viewing motherhood as a calling from God. A calling is something we approach with a sense of destiny. We recognize its significance and pursue whatever preparations are needed to ensure our success. We are aware of the privilege of being asked to fulfill this special task, knowing that our reputation or future opportunities depend on how well we are able to perform it.

We typically think of people being called to positions like pastor, missionary or evangelist. Some are called to teach in the church's children's ministry. Some sense a call for music or youth ministry.

Few mothers would describe their relationships with their children as a calling. Motherhood, after all, is more natural—not something that is significant, divinely inspired or special. Right? Wrong!

Motherhood is a position of eternal significance. This is because mothers can help their children embrace a vibrant, deepening relationship with Jesus Christ that culminates in their fulfilling *His* calling on *their* lives.

This goal is not attained easily. We will discuss more of the practical details of our children's commitment to Christ in a few chapters, but the mother who has this kind of expanded vision knows that no one can influence her children for the Kingdom of God the way she can!

The second obstacle to effective motherhood is being overly influenced by worldly philosophies. Consider the following New Testament warnings against placing our confidence as Christians in worldly wisdom:

> Do not conform any longer to the pattern of this world, but be transformed by the renewing of your mind. Then you will be able to test and approve what God's will is— his good, pleasing and perfect will.   Romans 12:2

> See to it that no one takes you captive through hollow
> and deceptive philosophy, which depends on human
> tradition and the basic principles of this world rather
> than on Christ.   Colossians 2:8

Today's mothers are prey to various philosophies. We want to do a good job of raising our children. We want to avoid the mistakes our parents' generation made with their permissiveness and trying to meet our needs with "things." It is natural to be eager and to hear and learn from others, but we must be careful of the advice to which we expose ourselves.

In considering the input of others, Benny and I consider two criteria. First, can I support this counsel with biblical principles? Does it violate any scriptural guidelines? Second, can this person point me to fruit in the lives of others for the advice he or she gives? These two simple guidelines have protected us from being influenced wrongly by those who do not share our views or our commitment to the Bible.

The third obstacle to effective motherhood is having had inadequate role models and unpleasant childhood memories.

A professor of human development at Harvard quoted in *U.S. News & World Report* (March 25, 1985) emphasized the influences of the home—and especially the mother/child relationship—in shaping our thinking and behavior:

> The home is the most important factor in the develop-
> ment of children ... it shapes the children's beliefs
> about themselves. In the first six years children believe
> that some of the qualities of their parents belong to
> them. A girl with a kind, nurturing mother will conclude
> that she has the same qualities. That belief is going to

help her. If her mother has the opposite qualities, she
may think that *she* is bad. It's harder for [an adult]
woman to conclude that she is good, despite real-life
successes, if she started with a negative identification.

The potential for influence over our children should drive
us to God for grace and wisdom! We can experience the
thrill of influencing our children for good or the heartbreak
of influencing them for evil. The potential for both resides
within each of us. Only dependence upon and obedience to
God will cause our influence to be positive, for anything
good in us comes only by His grace.

If you are among those women who encountered rejection, abuse or lack of affection and acceptance in your childhood, you may be in need of the healing touch of God. Only
He can help you forgive those who hurt you and protect you
from duplicating those hurts with your own children. You
may want to turn to a leader in your church or a trusted
friend to help you through this process.

I have been blessed with a wonderful mom who valued her
relationship with her children as a high priority. Her love,
acceptance and many sacrifices continue to provide an excellent example for me to follow. Yet even having a good role
model hasn't exempted me from dealing with character
flaws. I am tempted frequently to be impatient, for example,
such as when interrupted by the constant and seemingly
insignificant requests of the children. Sometimes I'm down-
right moody.

This is where I desperately need the input and help of my
friends. We all need friends from whom we don't hide our
weaknesses. They know us—good and bad—and love us
anyway: women with whom we can discuss the challenges of
motherhood without fearing their rejection or ridicule; and

friends we can trust to help us with our attitude problems.

I called such a friend recently to chat. The discussion turned to some ways in which I felt I had been letting our four-year-old Janelle "off the hook." I had become weary in dealing with some behavioral challenges in her—specifically, her outbursts of anger at her siblings and her frequent interrupting. These were things she was well aware were unacceptable. I knew that they would not be dealt with apart from my consistent discipline and encouragement, yet I felt I needed someone's help and accountability.

It felt good to be "known" by someone. I felt free to admit I had been selfishly inconsistent in dealing with Janelle—that I had lost faith that she would overcome these problems. Our discussion helped bolster me to continue to work on these character flaws in my little girl. I hung up the telephone with a fresh awareness of my need for other mothers with whom I could share my weaknesses and receive inspiration to "press on" in my relationship with my children.

Do you lack this kind of interaction with other women? The best way to find them may be to become involved in a church that shares your vision for successful family life. These kinds of relationships take time—sometimes years—to develop. Yet the benefits of having close friends who share your commitment to the Lord and inspire you to excel are well worth the effort.

The final obstacle to effective motherhood that many women face is an inability to identify and overcome areas of selfishness. For me, this has been the most challenging aspect of my pursuit of excellence as a mom.

There is no doubt that a mother has myriad responsibilities. I would venture to say, however, that all we do requires one common quality: unselfishness. Nearly everything a mother is called to do involves service to others. Selfish attitudes quickly prohibit even the most caring mother from excelling.

Many of us assume that because we are dutifully fulfilling our responsibilities, we don't have a problem with selfishness. The stay-at-home mom can be especially prone to this deception because she has chosen to leave her job to care for her children—surely an act of unselfishness. I was one such individual.

At age 23, I turned down a promotion in the company I was working for to prepare for the birth of our first child. Leaving the job was not difficult. I had always looked forward to having children and knew I would want to stay at home with them. My co-workers were surprised at my decision and even expected me to return after I had gotten full-time motherhood "out of my system." I was determined to prove them wrong. I knew that motherhood had a lot more to offer me than any position I could hold in the company. Plus, we had been trying to conceive for three years and there was no way I could have left my very wanted baby in someone else's care all day every day.

Adjusting to a new baby was more challenging than I had expected. With the exception of my mother and sister, I had no relationships with other mothers. I wasn't becoming the excellent housekeeper I assumed I would be. I lacked the self-discipline to organize my time wisely, and found that simply keeping the laundry done took more skill than I imagined. There were days when I ate my peanut butter and jelly sandwich in my nightgown—visualizing bygone days when I was smartly dressed and enjoying lunch at a nice restaurant with friends from the office.

When Joshua was just sixteen months old, we brought newborn Jaime home from the hospital with colic. Within weeks I was a total mess. Motherhood was much harder than

I had ever dreamed. In the office I had felt a sense of accomplishment. I was appreciated. I received a weekly paycheck that allowed for frequent dinners out, which we could no longer afford. I still had a deep sense of conviction that my place was at home with my children, but it was hard to uncover so many areas of incompetence.

Looking back, I now view that season as an important one in my Christian maturity. It revealed prideful assumptions that being a mother and homemaker would come easily for me. It helped me better to understand the desire many women have to return to the work force after childbirth. It forced me to pursue a more intimate relationship with the Lord as the source of my strength, vision and wisdom for motherhood.

Over time, I began to see that most of my inadequacies boiled down to selfishness in my life. This me-centered attitude manifested itself in various ways. I sometimes resented the inconveniences and interruptions—a drink of water while I was talking on the telephone, a hungry newborn who I thought would be sleeping through the night by now, a toddler with wet training pants for the third time in a day. I would become impatient or harsh with the children, something I said I would never do in those years of early marriage before we had children. In short, I simply wasn't the kind of mother I had expected to be.

Some might suggest that such frustrations are normal reactions rather than evidence of sinful attitudes, yet I knew that Paul's exhortation in Philippians 2:3 to do nothing from selfishness was clear. As a friend once said, *nothing* in Greek means just that—nothing.

Seeing my selfishness didn't cause me to feel condemned; instead, it gave me hope for change. If my ungratefulness, impatience, harshness and resentment were sinful, then I could confess my sin and appropriate God's grace to change. If not, I had only years of such reactions to look forward to. I chose the former.

I wish I could say, thirteen years later, that selfishness is no longer an issue in my life. Unfortunately, I am still tempted with selfish reactions and attitudes to which I too often succumb. The difference, however, is that my motives are revealed more quickly by the Holy Spirit and I am better able to resist the temptation. I am not always successful, but I am doing better than in those early years of motherhood. Again, my goal is not perfection but progression.

Maximizing Our Influence

Dealing with the above obstacles frees us to maximize our position of influence in our children's lives. Differing gifts and personalities allow for a variety of ways in which we can provide a positive influence for our children, yet there are four common areas we all share and can work together to enhance:

- Passion for God and involvement in His Church—we can show by our worship, by personal pursuit of God in prayer and devotions, and by active involvement in a local church that serving the Lord and seeing His Kingdom advanced is our greatest joy.
- Fulfillment in our roles in the home—we can model servanthood in our relationships with husband and children; inspire them to value family life; give the best of our time and creativity where it matters most; approach our duties responsibly.
- Commitment to resist worldliness—we can be content with our belongings; provide an example in our choices of entertainment (television, movies, etc.);

and generally exhibit love for eternal things over tem-
poral pleasures.
- Humility—we can become comfortable with asking
  for forgiveness from our families and others; be open
  with others about our personal weaknesses; solicit
  others' help and input to overcome character deficiencies; value others' thoughts and opinions.

Like me, you will fail at times. God's grace and forgiveness
are available to us when we are selfish, harsh, lazy or proud.
We must resist the temptation at such times to feel
condemned—"I'll never be the kind of example my children
need!" Making progress in overcoming sinful attitudes is the
goal. Our children will benefit from our efforts to grow.
Sometime down the road—maybe even sooner than we
expect—we may look back and see just how far we've come.

And remember, our influence as mothers isn't limited to
our children. The example we provide for them will, in turn,
significantly determine the way in which our grandchildren
will be influenced. Generations to come may actually be
affected by the way in which we train our children.

What other job has such potential?

13
Modeling the Fatherhood of God

Benny

Sheree and I were sitting in our living room talking with an engaged couple. It became clear that they needed to deal with some critical issues, not the least of which was their inability to control their physical desire. As the discussion progressed, we also understood why this young woman had difficulty resisting affectionate advances, despite her seemingly heartfelt desire to walk in purity. She admitted tearfully that she had not felt pure since age eleven when her father began to make incestuous advances toward her. The horror culminated in an abortion five years later at age sixteen.

Although not everyone has experienced the tragedy this young woman has, still many adults find it hard to love and accept God as their Father due to a dysfunctional relationship with their dads. A lack of genuine fatherly affection, love, initiative and care prevents them from fully enjoying these aspects of their relationship with God. Their eternal destinies as Christians are sure, yet they lack a sense of security and joy in the Fatherhood of God.

Think about it: The God of the universe is our Father! And He has placed on our shoulders an enormous responsibility. It is up to us as men to create a model of fatherhood that will help our children hunger to know their heavenly Dad.

For most of us, the problem isn't a lack of desire. We long to provide the best care for our children. No, we suffer from lack of training. We invest time and money preparing for a successful career, but how many of us pursue training for fatherhood? This, we presume, comes as a natural part of our manhood.

Actually, admitting this lack was easy for me. During my teenage years, I had no desire to become a father. My goal was to follow in my older brother's footsteps—stay in college as long as I could. Then, at about age thirty, I might settle down and marry someone who would be content with a small family. What little exposure I had to children convinced me that I was not cut out for life with whining, demanding people who made you lose sleep and money.

Then I met Sheree and, later, the Lord. Suddenly, thirty seemed like a long time to wait to get married. My growing desire to serve God in some way made years of hanging around college a waste of precious time. After all, there was a lost world to save and who could better accomplish that than me! (God was faithful to reveal my pride some years later.)

My high school sweetheart and I were married at age eighteen. In fact, I spent spring break of my senior year in high school on our honeymoon because my mother suggested we not wait. (I'm sure she was concerned that waiting would mean losing nice, well-mannered Sheree!)

After several years of college and a lot of necessary growing up on my part, we decided to start our family. The love Sheree and I shared and God's dealings with me—exposing selfishness and wrong attitudes about family life—caused a change in my heart concerning children. Three long years later, Joshua Michael was born. The joy and pride I felt when holding him for the first time flooded my being in a way for which I was unprepared. Within a few short weeks I was emotionally bound to this little man in a way I could never have imagined. I looked forward to his waking hours. I hurried home from school or work, anticipating his smiles and giggles. I enjoyed looking into his face and seeing myself.

In addition to the bond I felt with my son, I began to experience a fresh awareness of God as *my* Father. *Could God possibly love me as much as I love Josh?* I would wonder. *Does He long for my good as I long for my son's? Could He enjoy our relationship as much as I enjoy my relationship with Josh?* Over the years I learned that everything I cherish about my relationship with my children, God cherishes about His relationship with me . . . and more. I began to gain new revelation of the love and acceptance of God, my Father. One of the many results has been an intense desire to do my best at modeling the love of my Father to the children He has entrusted to my care.

This is not to say I don't feel inadequate as a father. You probably do, too. The responsibilities of providing for a family and raising your children can be overwhelming at times. You probably want to excel in your relationship with your children, but you feel ill-equipped to place family commitment above climbing up the corporate ladder. Or, like many young fathers today, maybe you are content to be involved minimally in your children's lives, leaving the nurturing to your wife—at least until they get old enough to relate to you on a more adult level.

I am a testimony to the power of God to change a man's

life. Aside from the fact that we now have a large family, something I used to think I didn't want, I enjoy a warm and loving relationship with each of the children. I can't imagine life without them. With the addition of each child, I have seen God expand my capacity for love and deepen my desire to overcome the self-absorption that thwarts my effectiveness as a father. God can help us overcome any wrong ways of relating to our children and enjoy a fulfilling home life.

Sheree and I have discussed many ways in which we can grow in our effectiveness as parents. I would like to focus on three key aspects of our role as fathers—demonstrating the father heart of God, becoming a "gatekeeper" and building family memories.

The Father Heart of God

One of the outstanding truths that singles out Christianity from all other beliefs is that our God is living and interactive. He has a personality. We can know Him personally. Jesus taught the disciples to pray, "Our Father who art in heaven," not, "O great influence in the sky." One of Jesus' primary missions was to reveal the Father to us (Matthew 6:4, 6–8, 14–15; 7:11). In fact, it was Jesus' acknowledgment of God as Father that motivated the Pharisees to take His life (John 6:39–40).

This Father-child relationship is one of the great comforts of Scripture. Like Jesus, Paul referred to God as "Abba," which literally means "Daddy" (Mark 14:36; Romans 8:15). Old Testament prophets spoke often of God as Father. Malachi underscored the significance of fatherhood by prophesying that the restoration of fathers' hearts to their children was a sign of the coming day of the Lord and ultimately the restoration of a nation (Malachi 4:5–6).

Imagine our President calling his advisors and experts

together to come up with solutions to the complex ills of our nation. Hour after hour, various individuals would offer intricate and well-thought-out proposals. Many of their ideas might be sound and helpful, yet expensive and difficult to implement.

"Sir," one man finally suggests, "I feel the solution to our nation's problems is a simple one. Our families need to become strong and healthy again. Fathers need to take their responsibilities seriously. We must use our time and resources to help them love and care for their children."

We can only imagine the response to such a simple answer. And yet this is the solution God saw for His hurting and distraught people. Maybe that's why God sent prophets instead of experts!

Linking the health of a nation to the health of its families may sound overly dramatic until you consider the influence of the father-son relationship in three of recent history's most powerful dictators. Joseph Stalin's father was an alcoholic who died in a brawl when Joseph was eleven years old. (His mother later sent him to seminary, where he developed an abhorrence for religion.) Mao Tse-tung had a violent father who beat him frequently and was the unfaithful husband of three wives. Adolf Hitler was illegitimate and he left home at age fourteen with intense hatred for anyone in authority.

I am not suggesting that the fathers of these men are entirely responsible for their sons' ideologies. It is noteworthy, however, that each of these men lacked a strong and loving relationship with his father. We can only speculate how different their lives—and those of countless others—might have been if they had had love and positive influence from their fathers.

We have not made much progress in this country in valuing a person's home life above his visible gifts or his career successes. We are basically a society that honors ability over character. Athletes, singers or politicians receive our applause even when their personal lives and families are suffering. Many suggest that what happens off the field or stage is none of our business. Could it be that our clapping, encouraging and financial backing are only making it easy for these individuals to sacrifice themselves and their families to perform for us, their fans?

As fathers, we must refuse this mentality of evaluating our success in life by how well we "perform"—the kind of house or car we own, the amount of our salary or the university from which we graduated. We must measure our success in this life by our abilities in areas of much more significance than these—our spiritual maturity, the depth of godly character in our lives, and our competence as husbands and fathers. For in these important areas lies the true test of our maturity and success.

Why is this so? Men can acquire possessions and job titles simply by knowing the right people or investing enough time and money in a good education. It requires character, however—things like patience, unselfishness, kindness and humility—to become spiritually and relationally mature. Developing such qualities equips us to model the father heart of God to our children.

One of the greatest illustrations of God's heart of fatherhood is found in the parable of the Prodigal Son (Luke 15:11–32). You probably remember that the father had two sons. The younger son was lured by the world and wanted to get out on his own. He requested his share of the inheritance, to which his father agreed. He left home and quickly squandered his money on wild living. Suddenly everything started to go wrong. A famine struck the land. He ran out of money.

Things got so bad that his hunger almost drove him to eat the food of the pigs he was hired to care for.

He finally realized that he would be better off working for his father as one of his servants. At least he would have food and shelter! As he made the long journey home he rehearsed what he would say to his dad. He would admit his sin and humble himself, hoping his father would have mercy on him.

While he was still a long way from home, his father saw him in the distance. He had good reason to begin to rehearse what *he* was going to say to this rebellious, selfish lad! Yet his love for the son he thought he had lost overwhelmed him, causing him to run to his son to embrace and kiss him. At his son's request to be hired as a servant the father called his servants and said:

> "Quick! Bring the best robe and put it on him. Put a ring on his finger and sandals on his feet. Bring the fattened calf and kill it. Let's have a feast and celebrate. For this son of mine was dead and is alive again; he was lost and is found."   Luke 15:22–24

This heartwarming story could easily end here, but it doesn't. Remember, the man had *two* sons. The elder son had remained with his father during his younger brother's escapades. In fact, he was in the fields working when little brother decided to show up. He was obviously bitter and confused.

"I've been the faithful, loyal son," he pouted. "I've always obeyed him and I've slaved for years to keep this place running smoothly. Has he so much as offered me a little goat to roast to share with some friends? No! And yet my selfish little brother can come home after spending his inheritance on prostitutes and loose living and *he* gets a party!"

I can identify with both of these sons. Before my conversion I did my share of wild living, which culminated, as I mentioned earlier, in a three-year sentence to a boys' penitentary. Mercifully, the judge suspended the sentence, placed me on three years of probation, and warned me that any unlawful activities would require that I fulfill any time of the remaining sentence in jail. (God has a great sense of humor. Ten years later this same judge became an elder in the church I pastor!)

I can also relate to the older brother. I would probably have shared his bitterness and frustration over the circumstances. I certainly wouldn't have been the first to offer to kill the calf I had been caring for to throw him a party! I would have found little comfort in my father's saying, "Son, please don't be upset. You know how much I love you and that everything I have will be shared with you. I'm just so glad that your brother is back. It was almost as if he died and has come back to life. Isn't that worth celebrating?"

"Can't say that it is," I may have thought, thinking that at least his death would have rid Dad and me of a lot of headaches.

This story is not just one of the love of a father for his wayward son. It offers a picture of the love of God for you and me. He is the father and we are the sons. What are some of the lessons we can learn from this vivid illustration of the father heart of God that we can implement in our relationship with our children?

1. *Be men of integrity.*

The younger son left because his father would not allow him to pursue his worldly desires at home. Likewise, we must model and require high standards of behavior and conduct in our homes. This requires a commitment to integrity, not requiring our children to uphold standards we are unwilling to model for them.

A commitment to integrity requires evaluating and then avoiding any activities or influences that could have a negative affect. This could happen directly (watching unwholesome television shows or movies with them) or indirectly through our example. The example we provide in our activities, entertainment, morals and relationships will influence our children for good or evil—and is a test of our integrity as fathers.

2. Have faith for their future.

Why did the father notice his son approaching from far away? Could it be that he was watching for him? I have to wonder if this concerned father had been hoping for his son's return, looking down the road day after day until he finally recognized something about the approaching figure. What a picture of God's eager desire for us to be restored to right standing with Him!

Likewise, we must persevere through any anxious seasons with our children. By faith we can look forward to their success and maturity.

Sheree's mother, Elsie, is a testimony to the faith and love of a parent for a wayward son. As a young teenager, Jon decided to forsake his Christian upbringing for a lifestyle of parties, drinking and drugs. Over the years, Elsie persevered in prayer. She confronted Jon's rebellion toward God regularly and refused to allow him to use drugs or alcohol in their home, yet she faithfully communicated her love for and acceptance of him. His conversion two years ago ended some fifteen years of her faith being tested.

Your need for faith may not be so dramatic. Maybe you need faith for a toddler to overcome temper tantrums or a school-aged child to become responsible and respectful.

Consistent discipline and instruction, coupled with faith, is the necessary strategy.

3. *Don't show favoritism.*

Outwardly, the brothers in the parable seem very different. One was responsible and hard-working while the other was frivolous and undependable. A deeper look reveals similar wrong motives in both: pride and selfishness. The younger brother expressed his sin in obvious ways through lust and greed. The older brother displayed his sin by being self-centered, jealous and bitter.

We might be tempted to address one child's rebellious behavior and tolerate another child's bad attitudes because of his outward compliance. This can lead to favoritism— giving more of our time, affection and acceptance to one child than another. As we discussed in chapter 9, both behavior and attitudes are equally important. The Prodigal's father responded lovingly to both his sons, which was evidence of equal acceptance and commitment.

4. *Believe the best.*

Why was the father so willing to receive his rebellious son? The son had a repentant heart. The older brother did not understand this. He continued to focus on his sibling's irresponsible departure, but the father saw his humble return.

As fathers, we sometimes find it difficult to accept our children's sorrow as genuine, especially when they've just been corrected for the same offense for the third time in an hour! We must communicate, however, that we believe the best of them, knowing that the wrong will most likely be repeated again soon—especially by young children.

I wish I could say that I model the principles above on a consistent basis. Although I have a conviction against disciplining them in anger, I too often communicate my frustration or lack of acceptance by my strained countenance or harsh words. Sheree calls it my "general's spirit"—that rushed or irritated feeling that motivates me to bark out commands or make sure they know how inconvenienced I am through an unexpected spanking. Fortunately, despite my failings, God gives me encouragement. It often comes through my children and shows me that a foundation of acceptance is being built into their lives.

When Joey was a toddler he had a unique way of responding to our discipline sessions. As I would rehearse with him the reason for his spanking, he would begin gently to stroke my face. "Yes, I know why I need a spanking," he would say as he rubbed my cheek.

At first I wondered if this was a manipulative way of delaying or avoiding the spanking. Then I questioned whether or not he was taking his spankings seriously enough. Over the months I began to see that neither concern was necessary. My son was simply expressing the security he felt in our relationship. Spankings didn't cause him to cower or withdraw from me emotionally because he was confident of my love for him. At times, as he would stroke my face, I would have to hold back the laughter and resist the urge simply to hug him and forget the whole thing. At age six, he no longer expresses his security in this way. I miss it.

Helping our children be secure in our relationship with them is crucial. Protecting them from a performance-oriented relationship is equally as critical in modeling the father heart of God to them. The Prodigal's father did not relate to his sons based on their external performance, but on their position as his sons. How many children face the pressure to perform well in order to gain their fathers' approval and attention? Such pressure motivates them to strive

for a better report card, to score more touchdowns, to practice the piano longer, to read the Bible more frequently.
Such things are, in and of themselves, good. Doing them to
bless or please us is one thing, but for children to be motivated because they fear our rejection or losing our love is
tragic.

Consider the reaction of God at Jesus' baptism (Matthew
3:13–17). When Jesus came up out of the water, the Father
declared: "This is my Son, whom I love; with him I am well
pleased" (verse 17). This was spoken at the beginning, not
the end, of Jesus' ministry. He had performed no miracles,
taught no crowds, confronted no hypocrites. What, then,
was the basis of the Father's pleasure and love? Jesus had
simply been an obedient son and a faithful carpenter.

Becoming a "Gatekeeper"

The second aspect of modeling the father heart of God to
our children is protecting them from influences that could
steal their spiritual passion. As I mentioned earlier, a friend
of mine called this having a "gatekeeper's mentality" (see 1
Chronicles 9:17–27).

The Levites, as gatekeepers, guarded several key areas of
the Temple to ensure that nothing unclean would enter and
jeopardize the people's meeting with God. The gatekeepers
protected the rooms and treasuries from theft, loss or unwholesome influences.

The implication to us as fathers is clear. We have the
responsibility to guard our children from those influences,
activities and relationships that could jeopardize their hunger for God. Such negative influences often cause a loss of
innocence, immature character development and spiritual
apathy.

Our interaction with other parents has shown that a minority of us invest the time and energy necessary to investigate our children's friends, coaches, entertainment, music and other powerful influences that can subtly affect their relationship with the family and, ultimately, the Lord.

Fear of being misunderstood as an "overprotective parent who is depriving his children of fun" is a weak excuse for allowing our children to be exposed to people and things that can steal their desire for God. Balance is certainly important. For instance, we do not want our children to be withdrawn socially, but neither should we be manipulated by some mythical need for them to be "socialized" by their peers.

How can we exercise our responsibility as the gatekeeper of our "temple"—the home?

First, we can monitor our children's relationships. During the toddler years, children begin to derive immense enjoyment from being with other children. By about age six to eight, they develop a legitimate need for a few friends with whom they can spend regular time and cultivate close relationships. It is at this age that peer influence becomes obvious. They want to act, dress and have the same toys as their buddies. By the pre-adolescent years, peer influence progresses into the next stage, peer dependence. The most obvious characteristic of peer-dependent young people is that they value their friends' opinions over their parents'. This craving for the attention and acceptance of their friends often leads to compromising the standards with which they were raised.

The potential danger for our children is obvious. Many a Christian parent can attest to their heartbreak of wishing they had monitored more closely the social influences of their children. Those of us who are parents of young children screen carefully the influence of other children. Our goal is not to isolate our children from interaction with families who don't share our values. Rather, our intent should be to protect our children from exposure to peers whose influence can, in a short time, undo those values that we are working hard to cultivate in them. We will discuss this further as it relates to preparing for the adolescent years.

The second way in which we can act as a gatekeeper is by choosing wholesome social activities for our children.

Every father wants his children to have fun. Our desire to allow fun, however, should not be more important than the potential consequences of exposing them to unwholesome activities. Two examples will help to illustrate this point.

Today's movies—even those that are marketed for children—are often full of messages that can subtly contradict Christian values. Fathers are often depicted as spineless and mothers as overbearing. The children are frequently deceptive, argumentative or manipulative, and sibling relationships are characterized by unkindness and competitiveness. Believing that our children are unaffected by such influences suggests a lack of knowledge of the power of the media. Exposing our children to it is a high price to pay for a few hours of good popcorn and family togetherness.

Team sports can pose another problem. Many coaches are responsible, loving and concerned about the feelings and well-being of children. Others, however, are selfish, foulmouthed and overly competitive. We must choose adult influences that will provide a positive model for our children, even though the individuals may not be Christian. We must also resist the temptation to assume our seven-year-old is ready for team sports simply because he or she has reached the age requirement or because his or her friends are participating. Evaluating our children's readiness by their character development will protect them from having any negative qualities reinforced (such as being overly competitive, selfish, prideful or emotionally immature).

The final way in which we can exercise our position as a gatekeeper is in making wise decisions about our children's education. Our society for many years displayed the attitude that parents should not be involved in their children's education. Educators, after all, were trained professionals who could best meet scholastic needs. In recent years, however, educators have begun to see the consequences of this lack of parent-child-teacher involvement in the educational process. Now many educators are pleading for the help of parents in disciplining and monitoring the scholastic progress of their children. Yet even with these changes, few consider parents capable of teaching or making curriculum selections for their children. Recent battles throughout the country over "family life curriculum"—materials designed to teach children about sexual functions, sexually transmitted diseases and birth control—have surfaced this debate about whether educators or parents should choose what is being taught to children.

As our children's gatekeepers, we must be involved in the most consuming aspect of their time—their education. For us and a growing number of parents, this has resulted in the decision to teach our children at home. Even if you do not take this step, refuse to accept the opinion that you are unqualified to involve yourself in your children's education. Meet your children's teachers. Become involved in any parent-teacher associations in your children's schools. Ask to see the textbooks and reading material they will be using. Basically, make your presence known in your children's schools. When concerns about any of these issues arise, pursue the proper channels to express your thoughts. Be willing to make whatever changes are necessary to remove your children from any harmful influences.

Other activities require similar discernment. Our society is, in many ways, very different from the days when you and I were growing up. Music instructors, neighbors and Scout leaders cannot be blindly trusted as they used to be—nor can all the children who join in these activities. The effort, time and willingness to investigate and be involved in our children's social interests can be demanding. Gatekeepers have a high calling.

Building Family Memories

The third aspect of modeling the father heart of God to our children is building family memories with them. God demonstrated the importance of this aspect of fatherhood by instructing the nation of Israel frequently to build altars in remembrance of His love and faithfulness. These structures reminded the people of His involvement in their lives and provided a visible source of curiosity to younger generations who could then be told of the deeds of God.

In a similar way, our children need memories—mental "altars"—of our involvement in their lives. A point we mentioned earlier bears repeating here because it applies particularly to fathers. This is the myth that the "quality" of the time spent with children and not the "quantity" makes the difference.

Today's fathers have been duped into this line of thinking. We assume that spending the little time we have with our children wisely makes up for the large amount of time we are away from them. This, we think, will meet their need for time with Dad. We would do well to consider another option—increasing our success as fathers by investing more time interacting with our children.

A University of Michigan study researched the average amount of quality time parents spend with their children. It defined quality time as time spent exclusively playing with, interacting with or teaching the children. According to this study the average father spends eight minutes daily and fourteen minutes on weekends of quality time with his children. This adds up to approximately 68 minutes per week or 57 hours per year—which is less time than most men spend in one week on the job!

At work, quality work requires a large quantity of time. Why do we assume that quality family life doesn't? We won't build many altars with 68 minutes a week!

Building memories requires the willingness to sacrifice that which is the most valuable to us—our time. Time to toss a football in the front yard. Time to set the newspaper down and admire a crumpled, scribbled piece of artwork. Time to talk about problems with friends. Time to play a board game when we had hoped to watch our favorite television show. Time to listen to their fears and insecurities. One by one, such building blocks add to the altar of memories they will enjoy for years to come.

One significant way we can provide rich memories for our children is by having regular vacations. A surprising number of fathers do not see the importance of spending time away with their families. Many excuses surface: "I can't afford a family vacation"; "My job is too demanding"; "We always get bored and want to come home"; or "I can't stand hearing the kids bicker all week."

Family vacations do not have to be expensive. Some families we know go camping. Others stay at home, unplug the telephone and enjoy day trips and picnics together. Others, like ourselves, have generous friends who loan them beach houses or cabins for a week or two. Expense should never be prohibitive in enjoying undistracted time together as a family.

Our yearly vacation at Nags Head, North Carolina, provides our children with a wealth of fun experiences and warm memories. At age thirteen, Joshua remembers eleven years of riding go-carts, playing in the ocean, climbing the sand dunes, eating soft ice cream, flying kites and fishing. We are blessed to be able to use the same beach house every year, which adds to the excitement and fun of our "Nags Head home."

Planning is an important aspect to a memorable vacation. Many fathers think that their families should feel blessed simply because they were willing to tear themselves away from work for a week. This leaves Mom to secure the place, pack, plan activities for the children and do the hundred other details of a successful vacation. Poor planning often results in simply transferring normal activities to another location—which, for many families, means watching television together.

Planning does not come naturally to me. In fact, my idea of a great vacation is sleeping late, eating bacon and eggs for breakfast every morning, spending some time bodysurfing in the ocean, taking a nap after lunch and sitting in a comfortable lawn chair on the beach reading a good book.

My children, however, go to the beach with different things in mind. Their excitement has them up earlier than normal. The younger ones want to run back and forth hundreds of times into the water. The older ones want to spend hours riding the waves, playing football and building huge sand castles. Josh loves to spend leisurely hours fishing—especially at ungodly times of the day. Then there are sand dunes to climb, beach balls to chase in the wind, water slides to ride and frisbees to throw. (I'm getting tired just thinking about it!)

Accomplishing these things without collapsing after attempting to do it all in one day requires planning. Thinking the time through not only makes for a more peaceful week, but communicates to our children that our family vacation is special and significant. Something I added to my plans several years ago is spending each afternoon alone with one of the children. I might take one to eat ice cream and play miniature golf after lunch, another to a good children's movie and another for a walk through a mall with five dollars to spend on a gift of his or her choice. I thought I would miss my afternoon naps. I don't.

Family vacations are a significant way to build memories for our children. Other building blocks can be spontaneous but still communicate our love and availability. A friend of mine took his eight-year-old daughter on a "date." They dressed up for the evening. He took her for a manicure, purchased her a corsage and took her to dinner at a nice restaurant. Another friend surprised his young son with a last-minute fishing trip on a Saturday morning. Our Joey's fondest memory is when I woke him at ten P.M. to take him out for ice cream and to watch the end of a men's softball game. (This was quite an event for a five-year-old!)

As our children get older, our ability to make memories with them should not decrease. Rather, their age and maturity should create meaningful and lifelong additions to our altar of memories. I had one such experience with Joshua when he had just turned twelve.

The churches we are associated with sponsor yearly short-term mission opportunities. The purpose of the week of evangelism is to distribute Gospel tracts, perform drama presentations and invite people to various outreach meetings throughout the week. Joshua joined me for one of these weeks. About midway through the week, I was to "open-air preach" following one of the drama presentations. As I finished, I noticed Joshua approaching a man on a bench with a tract. I watched for the next several minutes as he read through the tract with this man, giving him an opportunity to respond to the Gospel. The man, I learned, professed to have already made a commitment to Christ. They spoke for a few additional minutes, shook hands and parted ways.

The memories we shared together that week—reaching out to unbelievers, seeing individuals become Christians and praying for people—was a memory both my son and I will cherish forever. It was a significant addition to the altar that began more than a decade ago with rocking my infant son to sleep.

These three aspects of modeling the father heart of God for our children can play a significant part in their growing hunger for God. Why? The love, care, protection, availability and joy that fulfilling these responsibilities expresses to them can lead to a strong desire to know the God who has equipped their dad to express these qualities to them.

As fathers, we have a unique role in shaping our children's concept of God. To accomplish this effectively requires being willing to deal with any obstacles that stand in our way—selfishness, greed, laziness or harshness. We must evaluate what is most important to us in this life. Is it accumulating wealth? Being promoted? Impressing our friends and family with the home we own, the car we drive or the title of our position on the job? Or is it raising children who will enjoy the kind of relationship with us that will create in them a desire to know God as their Father?

You may be wondering if I am suggesting that you can't have both a successful career and a healthy relationship with your children. It depends on how you define success and health. For many men a successful career requires great quantities of time away from their families. For others, a healthy relationship means that their children are not abusing drugs and are doing well in school. Such definitions do not uphold biblical principles.

I have had to think through my definitions of these terms. I hope you will do the same. Seeking God for direction in these areas has been costly. I have had to repent of the self-absorption and laziness that thwarts my effectiveness as a father. I am still learning to make the right choices when I am tired, frustrated or preoccupied with my adult world. I have to cry out to God for the discernment and courage I need to be a gatekeeper for my children—something that is hard work for me.

Remember the bumper sticker we mentioned: "The man who dies with the most toys wins"? Too many of today's status-conscious fathers live with this philosophy. I hope you agree with me that all of the toys a man can collect in this life don't compare with the fulfillment and joy that come from a strong and loving relationship with his family.

That, to me, is winning.

14
Faith for the Adolescent Years

Sheree

Liz is a mother in our church with two small children. While taking her son to swimming classes, she was able to spend time getting to know one mother of a three-year-old girl. Over the weeks of the class the woman began to confide in Liz about some of her insecurities as a mother. She was from a very wealthy family and had a successful career—all of which allowed her daughter to have anything a child could ever want, things like a child-sized electric sportscar. She told Liz that her job wasn't a financial necessity, but rather an outlet for her creative abilities.

Unlike a majority of today's status-seeking parents, this mother was willing to acknowledge that the "things" she gave her daughter in an attempt to feel better about the amount of time she spent away from her were harmful to her. She admitted that her daughter was selfish and ungrateful, almost as if the more she was given, the more she desired.

"Have you thought about how all of this will affect your daughter in her teenage years?" Liz inquired.

"Oh, Liz," she responded, "I know we'll pay for the choices we're making now, and I don't even want to think about it!"

Apprehension about parenting adolescent children is a common fear. Some months ago we were enjoying a family dinner in a restaurant when a young father approached the table. We chatted for several minutes and he asked about the children's ages. After we went down the line, quoting each of their birthdays, he exclaimed: "Oh, my! That means you'll have four teenagers at the same time! I sure don't envy you!"

For today's parents, much of our anxiety about having adolescent children is based on our own experience as teenagers. Being teenagers in the tumultuous '60s and '70s meant a lot of headaches and tears for many of our parents. To a more blatant degree than previous generations of teenagers, we were thrill-seeking, rebellious individuals, experimenting with the new freedoms of the "me generation" in the backseats of our parents' cars and in the homes of friends whose parents were out of town.

Few of us were willing to swim against the tide of peer conformity. We did, said and tried things we felt initially uncomfortable with simply because we longed for acceptance. We lacked respect for our parents, resented having to do household chores or care for younger siblings and had little appreciation for the things they provided for us. We attempted to deceive our parents into believing we were upholding their standards. This, we now assume, is the perspective of the average teenager. If so, how can we do anything but brace ourselves for some very challenging years ahead?

Today's parents can also be anxious about teenagers because we hear of the increasing stresses and temptations this generation faces. The media is full of alarming references to suicide (the rate has more than doubled since

1970), drug and alcohol abuse, pregnancy and crime among teens.

This chapter is not designed to provide answers for those parents already encountering challenges with teenagers. Fortunately, others have addressed these important issues. Our intent is to address the concerns of those of us with younger children who need faith for the upcoming adolescent years. We need faith not just to persevere through the challenges, but to prepare ourselves and our children in a way that will avoid some of the dramatic difficulties the teenage years often present.

E. Kent Hayes, a juvenile criminologist who has worked for 25 years with children with serious problems, underscores the importance of the early years of a child's life as protection from difficulties later. He writes in his book *Why Good Parents Have Kids:*

> Our care of the child from birth to six provides the emotional foundation that will affect his behavior through his life. We are setting the standard that will affect much of what [he thinks] of the world and what [he] think[s] of [himself].

Preparing for adolescence, then, begins early, long before age thirteen. All of the things Benny and I have discussed—developing our children's character; shaping their concept of God; disciplining them lovingly and consistently; motivating them to obey; providing proper role models; protecting them from harmful influences; cultivating their hunger for God—help to ready our young children for the teenage years. A teenager who is growing in character and becoming spiritually mature will more successfully avoid the snare of peer conformity and bondage to his or her emotions and drives.

Do you remember what it was like to wait until the night before a big test in school to begin to study? Cramming for an exam seldom produced the results of a more systematic approach begun days or weeks ahead of time. Cramming for our children's adolescent years—by waiting until they are nearly upon us before we invest the time in our children's training—is equally ineffective.

By God's grace, many parents we know are experiencing exciting results with their older children who were not trained in the ways we have suggested thus far. Benny and I hope this encourages those of you who may be in a similar situation. Yet the most effective way to prepare for the adolescent years is by starting as early as possible to train, discipline, instruct and provide a proper example.

Having faith for the adolescent years is not simply a stubborn refusal to believe our sweet little ones could become rebellious, argumentative or immoral teenagers, nor is it a false sense of security in the fact that we read them Bible stories and worship together on Sunday. It is a confident expectation that the time we are investing in their emotional, spiritual and character development will—by God's grace and help—protect them from the common pitfalls of adolescence and prepare them for usefulness to Him. This testimony from Lisa, the sixteen-year-old daughter of a couple in one of the churches with which we are affiliated, underscores the importance of this kind of investment in our children's lives:

> I've been blessed to have been raised in a Christian home by parents who care a lot for me. From early in my life, I've been aware of God's great love for me. As I became a teenager, I saw many things I could experience in the world and pushed aside the things I had

learned from my parents. I wasn't always strong enough to stand against temptation. I sometimes resented my parents because I thought they were too strict. But my parents' consistent standards and devotion to me brought me through. I still have temptations, but I've decided to give my remaining teenage years to God, allowing Him to mold and shape me into the woman He desires me to be.

There are many aspects of preparing for our children's adolescent years that we could investigate. Our relationship with our own children and the input of families who are experiencing outstanding results with their teenagers suggest that we focus on two keys to developing faith for our children's adolescent years. First is the importance of companionship in the parent-child relationship. Second is the issue of maintaining our children's innocence.

The Importance of Companionship

The adolescent years are usually characterized by a deepening desire for companionship. For most teenagers, this need is met by spending a majority of their waking hours with friends. Many parents cooperate with this. Some selfishly enjoy not having their teenager around the house, while others assume seeing little of their teenager is a normal part of adolescence. After all, we assume, teenagers need significant time with their peers.

And, in fact, an adolescent's desire for deepening friendships is partially developmental in nature. In other words, the transition into an adult world of responsible interaction with others requires certain social skills—being able to get along well with various personality types and having well-developed communication skills, for example. Ideally, these skills are designed to be cultivated in adolescence.

The difficulty comes when parents and teens do not view peer relationships as training ground for the future. Most teenagers, for instance, tend to avoid those who are unlike them by clustering with those who share their personality, taste in clothing, hairstyle and financial status. How, then, will they be equipped for future interaction with those individuals with whom they must deal in adult capacities?

Who can best meet our children's need for companionship and, at the same time, equip them with skills for successful adult relationships? We feel that this need can best be met by us, their parents.

A radical thought? Yes. Typically, parents and their teenage children are not thought of as companions. Few parents and teens would define their relationship as a friendship—enjoying spending time together, pursuing common interests, laughing together and feeling secure enough to share concerns or fears. Yet the teenagers we have known who emerged from adolescence strong in character and spirit are those who enjoyed open, loving companionship with their parents. This kind of relationship was described to us by a friend of ours with a thirteen-year-old son:

> Jeremy is fast becoming one of my best friends. We are starting to have a lot of common interests. We play golf and racquetball together. He comes with me on various trips. We go from laughing together to discussing important things that are happening in his life. Basically, we simply enjoy being together.

Benny and I are not advocating an overly familiar atmosphere in the home where children relate to their parents as their "buddies," thus lacking respect for them. In fact, our suggestion to parents of young people who lack respect for them is to cultivate that important foundation before the companionship between them is emphasized. During the adolescent years our training, instruction, correction and guidance will continue—and even deepen. For it is during the pre-adolescent years and following that we should intensify our relationship with our children into what the Bible would define as a "discipleship" relationship—meaning that our instruction and training take on a more mature and systematic approach in preparing our children for the respon- sibilities and independence of adulthood.

A proper approach to companionship with our children will not jeopardize our rightful position of authority, just as Jesus' relating to His disciples as friends didn't dilute His role as master and teacher (John 15:15). The goal of parental companionship is to build a strong bond of love and security that will establish us as our children's trusted confidants during the adolescent years.

One University of Illinois study reported in *Newsweek* showed that during the years from age ten to fifteen, a young person's time with his or her family decreases by half. This dramatic change in the parent-child relationships significantly affects our ability to communicate with and understand one another, two necessary characteristics of successful family life in the teen years.

To what is this drop in time with the family due? Benny and I feel that it is because peer relationships take priority over those of the family. In a given day young people are spending six hours in school with friends. After school, they may go over to someone's house or meet at the shopping mall. After dinner they spend time together on the telephone or invite some friends over to watch television. On the weekends parents hardly see their teens. At a time when young people would benefit from a deepening relationship with their family, peers are occupying more and more of their time.

Author and youth leader Josh McDowell has invested many years in teaching youths. In his books and seminars for parents, he underscores the importance of companionship and well-established lines of communication with teenagers. He suggests that attempting to enforce rules without a strong relationship often leads to rebellion.

This concept is relatively easy to understand. Consider your relationships with those authority figures in your life. It is much easier, for example, to comply with your boss's rules and requests when a relational bond is present—that is, when you feel appreciated, accepted and valued.

In a similar way, we parents make it much easier for our children to comply with our rules when we have worked hard on our relationship with them. This doesn't mean we tolerate wrong behavior or attitudes. We must continue instructing, correcting and reminding them in the areas of needed growth in their lives. We must also, though, take a sincere interest in their lives, being current on what is happening with them and generally cultivating our friendship with them.

One of the many reasons teens choose a group of peers to share their deepest concerns with is often because their relationship with Mom and Dad lacks this aspect of companionship. When they are feeling rejected, confused or unhappy, they turn to their peers for the comfort, advice or encouragement they need. Most teens look to their peers for decisions about everything—what to wear, whom to like, what music to listen to.

Benny took an informal survey of parents recently by asking them this question: "How many of you went to your parents first about personal concerns or questions during your teenage years?" In the room of several hundred people, only one individual raised her hand.

"Would you mind telling us why you were able to go to your parents for these things?" he asked the woman.

"Because I had a wonderful relationship with them, almost like a friendship," she said.

This is not to suggest that the goal of successful parenting is having teens who share their hearts exclusively with their parents. Healthy peer relationships and interaction are a necessary and rewarding aspect of adolescence. It does mean, however, that companionship with our children is essential to their ability to trust us with the confusing and often conflicting concerns of adolescence—questions about puberty, sex or career decisions; problems with friends; insecurities about their appearance; or confusion about the emotional and physical changes that are taking place in them.

An experience with Joshua at about age twelve alerted Benny and me to the importance of parent-child companionship.

Aside from weighing nine pounds at birth, Josh has always been of average size. In recent years, several of his close friends have begun to show some pre-adolescent signs of muscle development and weight gain. On several occasions he asked if we thought he was "too skinny" or wondered aloud about how much he had grown over the last year.

We began to wonder if Josh was experiencing some common adolescent feelings of inferiority about certain aspects of his appearance. One evening we decided to bring it up.

"Son, we have a question for you," I began. "If you could change anything about the way you look, what would it be?"

"Well, I'd like to be a little taller and heavier."

"Really? Why?" Benny asked.

"It just seems like a lot of my friends are bigger than I am.

When we play football, I'm afraid I'll get smashed," he said, smiling. We appreciated his good natured attitude and apparent comfort with our questions.

"Does this ever make you feel self-conscious, like other people wonder if you're younger than you are?" I probed.

"Maybe sometimes. I guess I do wish I looked older."

Joshua's open and honest answers to our many questions that night led to a nearly two-hour conversation. He was surprised to learn that feelings of inferiority are common among boys his age. We talked about ways in which we had each felt inferior as young teenagers and how we, too, had assumed everyone noticed those things we didn't like about our appearance. We dispelled some important misconceptions that night—that his self-worth was not dependent on how others perceived him or how mature he looked. We talked about the danger of self-consciousness and how it prohibits many young people from being able to give a proper amount of attention to meeting the needs of others. It was an emotional conversation at times—with all three of us expressing heartfelt feelings.

"It sure seems like I've been worrying about some silly things," Josh offered as our conversation began to wind down.

"We wouldn't say they're silly," Benny responded. "As we said, you're in a season of life when everything takes on new and different proportions. It's easy to think that how tall you are is a big deal, but we appreciate your humility to admit that there are more important things to concern yourself with, son."

We ended the evening with a time of prayer. We suggested that Josh ask for God's help in overcoming self-consciousness and together we thanked Him for our ability to discuss such issues freely.

This would have been a wonderful enough ending to a

significant conversation with our twelve-year-old. At the close of our prayer, however, he reached over to hug us both.

"Thanks, Mom and Dad," he said. "I can talk to you about anything."

Our hearts were full of thanks to God for the years spent building the kind of relationship with our son that would lead to evenings like this—friends sitting on the couch talking about important and personal issues together. Our prayer is that this aspect of our relationship with him will continue to deepen.

Friendships take time. Year after year of befriending our children—providing a listening ear, sharing seemingly insignificant joys and struggles, being available for play or conversation, looking for areas to encourage or affirm, making fun memories together—will help to build the kind of relationship we long to enjoy with our teenagers. Such a commitment may begin with making room for the games, cuddles and silly questions of a toddler, but it may someday produce an adolescent who wants to come to Mom and Dad with his hurts, questions and dreams.

Maintaining Their Innocence

The second important essential in developing faith for the adolescent years is helping to maintain our children's innocence. The temptations and harmful influences our children face are strikingly more dangerous than those today's parents encountered as teenagers. Today's young people are expected to take on the responsibilities of adulthood at an early age. Many come home from school to empty houses, often to care for younger siblings for hours until a parent arrives from work. Violent and sexually explicit images are readily available to them—through television, music, magazines, movies and interaction with peers in school. A growing number of schools, like some of those in our Washington, D.C., suburb, are beginning to install metal detectors at entrances or use police patrol to protect children from violent crime in the classroom.

Childhood is a treasured season of life. Yet, for many youngsters, the innocence of childhood is being swallowed up by a premature exposure to adult stresses and influences. As parents, we have the responsibility to protect our children from harmful people and situations.

Otherwise, if we adopt our society's philosophy that anything goes, we will undermine our children's passion for God and prevent them from walking in blameless and holy devotion to Jesus Christ. David speaks of the kind of commitment to purity that we should desire to see in our children in Psalm 101:2–4:

> I will be careful to lead a blameless life. . . . I will walk in my house with blameless heart. I will set before my eyes no vile thing. The deeds of faithless men I hate; they will not cling to me. Men of perverse heart shall be far from me; I will have nothing to do with evil.

Training our children early to take this radical kind of position will serve them greatly in the critical teenage years. Equipping them to embrace Paul's exhortation to "say 'No' to ungodliness and worldly passions, and to live self-controlled, upright and godly lives in this present age" (Titus 2:12) is the heart cry of every parent who is even mildly aware of the temptations our young people face each day. We must do our part to equip our children to "have nothing to do with evil."

Attempting to maintain our children's innocence does not mean we isolate them from the world. Still, as we would care for a young plant that must be properly watered and protected from extreme temperature changes, so we must guard our children from influences that could prohibit their ability to "survive" to spiritually mature adulthood.

Many parents minimize symptoms of worldliness in their children because "compared to many of their peers my children are doing great!" Others think, "My kids? Worldly? You should have seen *me* at their age!" As Christians, our standard of behavior and values is not the godless society in which we live, but God's Word. Comparing our children to unbelievers (ourselves as teenagers or their peers) is a wrong standard. As Paul said, "When they measure themselves by themselves and compare themselves with themselves, they are not wise" (2 Corinthians 10:12).

Many of us had to be rescued by God from addiction, perversion and rebellion—for which we are eternally grateful. Is this, though, what we want for our children? Do we want to bank on the fact that even if they "experience the world" they might still make a serious commitment to the Lord? What a waste of precious years of youthful energy and zeal! And the often permanent scars that sin leaves behind could jeopardize their fruitfulness to God.

Comparisons are dangerous. Our security should not be based on the perception that our children look, act and relate to us in a way superior to their peers, but that their attitudes, actions, behavior and example are pleasing to God. Our goal is that our children will be increasingly conformed to the image of Jesus Christ.

Here are some common concerns Christian parents face, with some corresponding thoughts for your consideration.

1. What if my child rebels against all our standards and rejects Christianity altogether?

As parents, we must base our standards in the home on biblical principles and guidelines. We cannot compromise or lower these standards for anyone, including our children. To do so would be disobedience to God. Children often rebel against high standards not because they resent them, but because of the way in which they are enforced (see chapter 10 on motivating your children by grace). Teenage rebellion and spiritual apathy are often the eventual manifestations of negative attitudes that went unaddressed in early childhood. Whatever the age of the child, rebellion must be consistently and lovingly punished. Fearing a child's rejection of Christianity should never cause us to compromise godly standards in the home.

2. I'm afraid my child will grow up resenting us because we are so "strict."

As a Christian, do you resent God's standards for attitude and conduct? Do you feel restricted by having to say no to adultery, murder, lying or stealing? Certainly not. Even though you may be tempted in these areas, you value obedience to a loving God who has your safety and purity at heart. You know that His motive is not to prevent you from having fun in life but to protect you from the consequences of sin. In a similar way, children who understand their parents' *motives* for their standards, to protect and prepare them for the future, learn to appreciate even strict rules. This comes through a balance of correction and affirmation. Even though they may experience seasons of resistance, like Lisa—whom you read about earlier—they will come to appreciate the standard and have greater respect for their parents.

3. I don't want my child to be too sheltered. Someday he'll have to deal with the real world out there!

Our goal is not to shelter our children *from* the world but to prepare them *for* the world. Just as a mother bird nurtures her young until they are ready to fly, so we must train and prepare our children for life in a world that is hostile to Christian values. Tossing them out of the nest prematurely can result in serious damage to their spiritual health. Benny and I have seen that children who are prepared and discipled adequately by their parents are able to function in a mature and responsible manner when the time comes to face the "real world."

4. I'm concerned that my teen won't know how to discern right from wrong on his own if I make all his decisions for him.

In a child's early years, parents are responsible for making his decisions. As he matures, however, the wise parent will slowly begin to entrust certain non-critical decisions to him. By the teenage years, a well-trained child will be equipped with the decision-making abilities needed to make discerning choices. In his book about adolescence, *All Grown Up & No Place to Go*, David Elkind, professor of child studies at Tufts University, discusses the difficulty teens face in making decisions:

> Teenagers, particularly young teenagers, have trouble making decisions. It is agony to decide what to wear, what to eat, sometimes even what to say. . . . The difference in this area is the amount of experience in making decisions; as a result of this experience the adult has required some rules and strategies for making decisions.

We make decisions for our children initially to allow them to benefit from our experience (the rules and strategies we have required over the years). As they mature and show they are learning from our example, we can then slowly trust them with making their own decisions. Our goal should be to release them as young adults, fully equipped to make wise, godly decisions. Our input over the years should prepare them for decision-making, not cause them to be irresponsible and wrongly dependent on us.

5. I don't want my child to become legalistic—focusing on externals as the way to please us and God.

As Christians, our obedience to God should be born out of our relationship with Him as Father, not from self-imposed pressure to gain His acceptance through our deeds. Likewise, our children's compliance and obedience should be a willing response to our love and acceptance of them. This is not to suggest that they will never disobey. They will disobey, at which times they should be firmly and lovingly punished. Concern that our children not become legalistic should not cause us to lower our standards, just as God has not adjusted His standards to accommodate our tendencies toward legalistic responses to Him.

6. I'm afraid my child will miss out on some fun things I enjoyed at his age if he isn't allowed to participate fully in various activities.

Benny and I are not promoting a "lock-your-child-in-the-house-and-restrict-all-his-activities" approach to parenting. We are, however, emphasizing parental respon- sibility to guard the influences and activities of children. As adults, we have memories that often involve "revisionist history." We remember the fun of adolescence and forget the pain, confusion and guilt.

Consider eighteen-year-old Kim's perspective on what she "missed" during her teenage years because of her parents' standards:

> As I look back on my early teenage years, I realize all
> the things I missed. I missed the pain and frustration of
> rebelling against my parents' rules and standards. I
> missed experimenting with drugs, alcohol and sex—
> which many of my peers were involved in. Actually, I
> *didn't* miss these things. I was spared from them by
> God's mercy and my parents' love and protection. I
> didn't have to pay the high price of giving in to peer
> pressure and worldly influences. I thank God (and my
> parents) for dealing with my heart so I didn't have to
> learn some lessons the hard way like many of my peers.

Notice that all of the above concerns are rooted in one thing—fear. Fear should not be the basis of any decisions about our children. The Bible has much to say about the consequences of adopting worldly values and being exposed to negative influences (see 1 Corinthians 6:19–20; 15:33; 2 Corinthians 6:14–18; Ephesians 4:17–24; Colossians 3:1–10). Faith—not fear—is our guide. Would it not be better to err slightly toward overprotectiveness than to expose our children to potentially destructive influences?

Yes, like every parent before us, we will all make mistakes. And as our children mature we must begin to release them knowing that they, too, will sometimes fail. Yet a child who feels his or her parents' deep love and concern will come closer to understanding. As a friend of ours who was going through some challenges with his teenager put it: "Son, you need to be patient with me. I've never had a sixteen-year-old before!"

Parent-Teen Conflicts

In the families with teenagers with whom we have had contact over the years, it seems that the majority of parent-child conflicts fall into five main areas: responsibility in the home, dress, hairstyle, entertainment and peer relationships (including with the opposite sex). We have already covered the first category. We now offer some suggestions to help you develop your personal standards as a parent in the other four areas.

1. *Dress.*

As we mentioned, preteens and teenagers are very aware of their appearance. They are eager to conform to trends down to the smallest details of how to wear their socks and what brand of sneakers to buy. These things associate them with a particular kind of peer group and affect their self-esteem.

We should not force our children to be "different" simply for the sake of being noticeably unlike their peers. They can be stylish without being indecent. Some basic guidelines for wardrobe are:

- Modesty—Not drawing attention to or exposing certain parts of their body.
- Appropriateness—Choosing the proper clothing for the occasion.
- Non-attention-getting—Avoiding dressing purposely to be noticed by others, especially the opposite sex.
- Stylish vs. trendy—Making purchases on genuine preferences and tastes rather than "what everyone else is wearing" (peer conformity).
- Acceptable use of money—Not placing financial pressure on the family for excessive or expensive clothes.
- Age-appropriate—Selecting styles that protect them from being viewed/viewing themselves as older than they are.

2. Hairstyle.

Our society is infatuated with hair. We wash it so much we have to use conditioners to keep it from drying out. We use chemicals to curl it and hot curlers to straighten it. We pay outrageous amounts of money to have it cut and blown dry. And we spend time daily primping and combing, using various gels and sprays to keep it in place, which means we have to repeat the whole process tomorrow.

Today's teenagers are not unlike us at their age. Their hair is an important aspect of their appearance. Their self-worth on a given day can have a direct link to whether or not their hair "turned out right" that morning. ("Oh, how silly," we think, as we yank out another gray strand!)

Here are some guidelines to consider in determining our children's hairstyle. It should

- Not be rooted in conformity to current trends (*everybody* wears their hair this way) when it is not becoming to them or acceptable to us.
- Not require an inordinate amount of time or expense to maintain.
- Be age-appropriate.

3. Entertainment.

Entertainment is a huge industry in our nation that has a dramatic influence over our children. Many of today's young people idolize those they see on television, at the movies and on album covers (or should I say C.D. cases!). We have already underscored the importance of taking our responsibility to monitor these things seriously. In establishing our standards, we can't be fooled into thinking that all forms of entertainment that are called "Christian" or "wholesome family entertainment" are necessarily appropriate.

The following guidelines are minimum considerations for establishing standards in these areas:

- Does it reinforce our standards of conduct and morality?
- Have I or someone I trust previewed this? If not, am I willing to watch/listen to this with my child to address any inappropriate or harmful issues?
- To the best of my ability to discern, would it be pleasing to God?
- Will it expose my child to sensuality? Introduce images he may not easily forget? Cause him to have harmful desires or fantasies? Instill fear?

4. Peer relationships.

Just as with adults, children have different levels of relationships that range from acquaintances to close friends. While you would be more concerned about your child's close friends than those with whom he has only casual contact, still adolescents can be acutely influenced by even casual interaction with their peers. It is important that these things be considered in all relationships between your children and others.

Ask yourself the following questions about your child's friends or potential friends:

- Are there character qualities in this friend that could inspire my child in areas of lack or weakness?
- Am I aware of/comfortable with the environment in which this friend is being raised and do his or her parents reinforce our basic standards, values and morals?
- Do I have an adequate ability to communicate with this friend's parent(s) to discuss any concerns, con-

flicts between the children, etc.? If not, am I willing to invest the time to build this kind of rapport with him or her?

- Would I be comfortable with allowing my child to spend time in this friend's home? Would I be concerned about unwholesome influences (movies, music, language)?
- Will this relationship meet my child's need for friendship without jeopardizing the priority of our relationships as a family? (We want to help our children avoid friends who will be possessive and demanding about spending time together.)
- Will this friend's influence (values, morals, activities) pose no threat to my child's Christian commitment?
- Considering the personality differences or ability to communicate between my child and this individual, is my child equipped to stand alone in defense of his or her values and morals if necessary?
- Does this child have the desire to "fit in" to our family life when he or she is around?

Being able to answer the above questions affirmatively indicates the potential for a rewarding peer relationship. Benny and I have found it helpful to discuss these kinds of issues with our children from a young age to help create in them an appetite for wholesome peer relationships that are pleasing to God.

In fact, the sooner we begin to establish and maintain good standards, the easier the teenage years will be. Our best bet is to start in the toddler years.

We were enjoying some time as a family recently at a nearby playground. Seven-year-old Jesse was watching several boys about his age playing basketball, probably hoping to be asked to join them. After a few minutes he came to sit with us on a bench.

"What's the matter, son, are you tired?" I inquired.

"No, it's just that those boys were using some bad words."

"Really? Well, thanks for making such a wise decision to leave."

This may seem like an insignificant little exchange, yet the long-term possibilities of his avoiding negative influences are exciting. A seven-year-old leaves the basketball court to avoid those who use vulgar or unkind language. At ten, he may begin politely to ask neighborhood friends who use offensive language to leave his yard. By sixteen, his well-developed commitment to right living gives him the courage to say no to an offer to attend a party with some friends because of the negative reputation of those who are hosting it.

Beginning to develop a strong relational bond with our small children will lead to a healthy companionship with our adolescents. High standards of conduct will produce teenagers who are equipped to avoid worldly temptation. This alone can give us faith for the adolescent years.

It may seem as though I have made this all sound very easy. Believe me, Benny and I know that the principles shared here take years of hard work, sacrifice, recovering from mistakes and lots of prayer. Yet we and other families we know are experiencing the joy of freedom from fear of our children's teenage years, as many of them have made the transition from childhood into adolescence with growing hunger for God.

We were blessed recently to hear Joshua's close friend, Andy, express the kind of heart for spiritual growth that we can pray for in our young people:

I would like to learn more about God's Word in the years ahead so that when I'm older I'll be more able to hear God's voice when He speaks to me about things. I also feel very unprepared to share the Gospel with people—so I need to be trained and equipped to do this. Someday I want God to use me to help to change some things in our world. But mostly I want to become all that God wants for me.

Our curiosity about the goals and concerns of members of the next generation—which prompted us to solicit the testimonies we have included in this chapter—was directed most keenly toward our own teenager. We talked with Joshua about his concerns and hopes for this fun but challenging season of life. What was he looking forward to? What were his goals and dreams as a young adolescent? In what areas did he desire our help in fulfilling these things? We thought it best to allow him to express his thoughts about our conversation:

I am really looking forward to my teenage years, mostly because I'll be able to learn how to drive! But also because I'll be able to grow stronger in the Lord and be able to preach the Gospel to people who probably wouldn't listen to a younger person.

I know that as I get older I'll have to make a lot of important decisions with my parents' help—like where to go to college, who to marry and what kind of job to get until I know what God's call on my life is. I want to learn how to make wise decisions.

When I was younger I wondered sometimes why my parents had certain rules, like not letting me play with certain children I thought were fun to play with. Then I saw that I was being influenced by their wrong attitudes rather than being a good influence on them. I want to continue to learn to choose my friends wisely. I think I can do this better now because I don't want to build close friendships with people who won't be a good influence. Then I'll have more boldness to share the Gospel with those who need a positive influence from someone their age.

I want to grow in pleasing the Lord and my parents. I know that the time my dad and I spend on Saturdays studying books together and talking will help to give me the wisdom I'll need. His advice is very important.

Being a teenager will be a lot of fun but I know that my relationship with the Lord and my family need to stay as the most important things to me.

If you have young children, begin now to anticipate their needs as future adolescents and then consider ways you can help build into them the qualities needed for their success. If you have older children in or approaching adolescence, consider having a similar conversation about their future as we enjoyed with the young people you have heard from here. Like us, you may discover some important ways in which you can help to see their concerns minimized and their dreams fulfilled.

Fear of their future can be greatly diminished as a new level of companionship and mutual commitment to holy living begins to emerge. Faith for our children's adolescent years requires having a vision for our future teens—vision that motivates us to pay whatever price is necessary to walk through these years with an ever-deepening commitment to our children as our priority.

And we may even find that they will respond like our daughter's twelve-year-old friend Sarah, the oldest of eight children:

During my teenage years I would like to help my parents more so they can have time to rest.

On behalf of parents everywhere, *Amen* to that!

15
Leading Your Children to the Lord

Benny

"Hi, Dad," Jesse called as he came into the house. "What are you doing?"

"Oh, I'm just getting some things together to wax the car. What do you need?" As I glanced over at him I couldn't help but notice how tall our six-year-old was becoming. It seemed like such a short time ago that he was crawling around under my feet.

"Nothing. I just wanted to tell you something."

"O.K. What is it?"

"Well, this morning I asked Jesus into my heart," he said matter-of-factly.

"You did? I sure want to hear about this. Let's sit down and talk about it."

For several years Jesse had been talking about becoming a Christian. Like most young children, his initial inquiries were

based on curiosity rather than genuine readiness to understand the Gospel, but in recent months he had shown an
awareness of his need to be forgiven for his sins. He seemed
to be approaching the desire to make a sincere commitment
to the Lord. Several days earlier he had even asked Sheree if
we could pray with him. We had neglected to follow through
on our commitment to discuss it with him over the weekend.
It seemed he had decided to handle things on his own.

"So tell me about this morning," I said as we sat down in
the living room.

"Well," he began, "when I woke up I started thinking about
becoming a Christian. I wished that today could be the day.
When I got out of bed, no one else was awake yet so I went
downstairs. While I was sitting there I decided to pray."

"Tell me about your prayer, honey."

"I remembered what you told me about asking Jesus to
forgive me from my sins, so I did that. Then I asked him to
come into my heart and make me a Christian."

"Why don't you go and find Mommy so we can talk about
this together? I know she will want to hear what you've told
me."

The three of us had a meaningful time discussing Jesse's
desire to become a Christian. It was obvious that our son
was going to pursue this commitment—with or without our
help. He had an adequate understanding of the Gospel, of his
need for forgiveness and of the seriousness of this decision.
To seal this memory, he prayed a sincere prayer of commitment to Jesus with us and the other children listening. It was
an emotional moment for us all.

What a joyous day when a child makes a heartfelt commitment to following the Lord! Few experiences in life compare with hearing your son or daughter repent of sin and
dedicate him or herself to following and serving Jesus Christ.

We have been privileged to pray with four of our six children to make this decision.

The goal of everything we have discussed thus far—shaping their concept of God; building respect, responsibility and responsiveness into their lives; disciplining them lovingly; cultivating their hearts for God; modeling His Fatherhood; and influencing them for good—is to see our children come into a personal relationship with Jesus Christ and fulfill His plan for their lives. Any other aspirations we may have for them, no matter how important they may seem, pale in comparison to these.

Sometimes it's hard to keep such long-term goals in mind for our children. This means we become easily discouraged when our training doesn't seem to be bearing fruit and easily heartened when we see progress. Our discouragement can prevent us from persevering through the challenges. Being wrongly content with the progress can deceive us into thinking our children are further along spiritually than they really are. Either extreme can frustrate our children's spiritual maturity.

It helps if we resist the temptation to place too much emphasis on either positive or negative seasons of spiritual interest in our children's lives. Just as we have ups and downs in spiritual appetite, so do our children.

Have you thought how we tend to develop a taste for that to which we are exposed regularly? I grew up eating my grandmother's homemade chocolate pies. Whenever a restaurant offered chocolate pie for dessert, I would try it, hoping it would taste like Mamau's. It never did. Sheree purchased every boxed pie on the market and tried many recipes to match the special taste and texture that characterized her pies. I had been spoiled by those pies, and nothing could match them. Then, after nearly eighteen years, we hit the jackpot! Sheree finally found a recipe that tasted like Mamau's chocolate pie.

Similarly, our children can develop a "taste" for the spiritual food they grow up enjoying. In a sense, they can be "spoiled" for the Kingdom of God. What I mean by this is that they can so appreciate the quality of their Christian upbringing that nothing else this world has to offer will satisfy them. Only the "real" thing will suffice—authentic Christianity that invades every area of their lives.

Oh, to know the details of God's purpose for our children and their generation! Reaching for this will help us through hard days when it seems this generation of young people is being quickly lost to Satan's ways. As the peers of those young people who are selling themselves to drugs, alcohol, premarital sex and greed, our children will be used best to arrest their attention to the things of God.

How can we instill in our children this vision for usefulness to God?

Giving Our Children a Vision

First, we must ask ourselves what our goals are concerning our children's spiritual development and then provide them with an example worth emulating. In short, we must do our part to cause them to hunger for the kind of walk with God that we enjoy.

One way in which we can do this is by recounting the blessings and deeds of God in our lives with our children. The Psalms are full of references to the deliverance and provision of God spoken by former generations for later ones. Psalm 44:1 says: "We have heard with our ears, O God; our fathers have told us what you did in their days, in days long ago." The chapter goes on to describe specifics of the protection and provision of God in former generations. This knowledge built hope for the difficulties the people were experiencing. "Rise up and help us," they cried, "redeem us because of your unfailing love" (verse 26).

Our children enjoy hearing that Sheree wasn't supposed to be able to have children and received the healing touch of God. They are inspired by how He has provided for specific needs in response to our prayers. They don't tire of hearing how He responded to our cries for help when someone in the family was sick, injured or in desperate need. And they love to hear how Jesus moved miraculously in Uncle John's life to bring him into a relationship with the Lord.

Being the right example may require a serious evaluation of our own relationship with God. We must ask ourselves some important questions:

- Have I experienced a genuine encounter with Jesus Christ, including repentance from my sin and a commitment to following and serving Him?
- Is my relationship with the Lord growing and deepening?
- Is there visible evidence of my Christian commitment in my lifestyle (activities and values) and in my relationships (Christlike attitudes and behavior)?
- Is my relationship with the Lord being walked out with other like-minded believers in a local church that emphasizes relationships and personal pursuit of God over attendance at meetings and religious rituals?
- Is my pursuit of God visible in the home, or is it limited to church services or crisis management?

Our answers to questions like these help us evaluate the extent to which our children are being affected and inspired by our Christian experience. If our walk with God is evident only by church attendance and a clean vocabulary, we should not be surprised if our children's spiritual lives are equally superficial. If our commitment to Him pervades every area of our lives, however, and is apparent in our lifestyle, relationships, church involvement and devotional life, we can have hope that our children will develop a similar hunger for intimacy with Jesus Christ. At times, having this kind of lifestyle can be costly.

Keith and Patsy are special friends of ours who have made some unique sacrifices for the sake of their family's spiritual health. Keith was a successful youth pastor in a growing church in Florida. He was loved by the teenagers and was gaining the respect and confidence of the leadership of the church. Years of Bible college training and "coming through the ranks" in his denomination were finally paying off. His future in ministry was bright. In fact, he was anticipating a welcomed salary increase after years of scraping by on a meager income.

But Keith and Patsy were restless. They were having some difficulties in their marriage and had no one in whom to confide. Keith's tendency to invest an inordinate amount of time and energy into the ministry was appreciated by his overseers and not seen as a detriment to his relationship with Patsy and their young daughter. And Patsy's spiritual dryness was undetected by those around her.

Keith then heard a pastor describe authentic Christianity in terms of a vital relationship with the Lord, involvement in a church that esteems successful family life and strong interpersonal relationships, and the importance of character over gifting in the lives of the leaders. Keith knew he and Patsy had some difficult decisions to make. His family's spiritual health was at stake. His strong desire was to see his child grow up experiencing Christianity that would affect every area of her life. This, he knew, would require help in their marriage, parenting and character development. Their choice was either to continue on in their position of ministry with little hope that their family life would improve, or to align themselves with those who shared their vision for New Testament church life and successful family relationships.

Keith and Patsy made a difficult decision, one that many did not understand. He resigned from his position in the church and they moved several hundred miles to become part of a church they felt would help them grow spiritually. Not that he had been offered a position on the church staff; rather, he accepted a position selling snacks to businesses, and later became a roofer. His and Patsy's passion to serve God motivated them to give up what most people would consider a prime way to "serve" the Lord—involvement in full-time ministry—to put themselves into a situation where their family life and personal relationships with the Lord became the priority.

Now, years later, both Keith and Patsy chuckle at the idea that their decision was a sacrifice. What they gave up does not compare, in their hearts, to what God has done. Their marriage is strong and healthy. Their relationship with their children is an example to all who know them. They are grateful for the ways their willingness to obey God will affect their children's future relationship with Him.

The cost to you may not involve relocating to another state; nevertheless, there will likely be a price to pay. It may be in time spent seeking God for ways in which your spiritual zeal has waned over the years or unconfessed sin has thwarted your passion for Him. You may need to consider evidence of any pursuits that are taking precedence over fervor for God and His Church. You may begin to wonder, too, if the church you are involved in is the best place for your family's spiritual and relational health. As hard as it may be, years from now the cost will seem minimal.

A second way we can help our children have a vision for usefulness to God is by expanding their awareness of God's efforts in the earth today. Most young people desire to give themselves to something "big." They want to feel that they are a part of something significant. Our generation fulfilled this desire at Woodstock or in marches protesting the Vietnam War and nuclear weapons. Our children can achieve this goal in a much more exciting way with our help: by throwing themselves into involvement in the Church.

By the Church I'm not speaking of the building where they attend services on Sundays. This is too limiting to the average young person who is looking for a meaningful cause to which he can give himself. Rather, I mean the Church as the people of God throughout the entire earth—people of every nationality, color and tongue.

Each spring we attend a conference that involves ten of our affiliated churches. Last year, Joshua was old enough to join us in the evening meetings in which some 2,500 people gathered for a time of worship and teaching. We noticed that Josh seemed to be enjoying it. He worshiped expressively and paid close attention to the speaker. After the meeting ended, we were interested in his comments.

"That was great!" he said. "It was exciting to be part of something so big! I can't wait till tomorrow night."

It was our son's response that reminded us of this need in young people to give themselves to that which entices and excites them. Their relationship with the Lord can take on new meaning when they are made aware of the expanse of their "Christian family." They begin to feel as though they belong to something of value and importance that surpasses

Sunday morning church attendance or involvement in the youth group.

Most young people do not have this view of Christianity. They see it as a once-a-week commitment rather than a relationship with God and membership in His family throughout the earth.

Brianna is the fifteen-year-old daughter of our friends Mike and Judy who has the kind of vision for her life that we desire to see in our children. In early 1990 her family left the comfort and security of their suburban home to begin a new church in Mexico City, Mexico. When asked to share her thoughts on the relocation, Brianna wrote:

> A lot of teens in this generation aren't very committed to the Lord. They don't have much of a heart to serve God. I'm not sure exactly what God has planned for my life . . . but I know that I'm going to be playing a part in the work down here—establishing a church and discipling other young people.

Eighteen-year-old Scott is involved in another church and shares Brianna's desire to be used in a significant way in his peers' lives:

> I believe God has called me to cross-cultural missions. A lot of kids are just disillusioned with church. It's not relevant to them. [My advice to my generation is to] be willing to trust in God and walk in His ways and you will have the adventure of your lifetime.

This sense of adventure is what young people are looking for! Young people like these easily resist temptations to give themselves to immoral or unwholesome activities because they live with a sense of mission and destiny.

In Brianna's and Scott's cases, as with other young people Sheree and I know who have a vision of usefulness to God, a key to their spiritual development is healthy communication with their parents. Many young people today feel awkward discussing spiritual things with their parents. They can interpret their parents' interest in or inquiries about their relationship with God as pressure to conform to Mom and Dad's Christianity. They feel their pursuit of God is their own business.

Although common, such an attitude suggests a deeper issue than an unwillingness to talk openly about their relationship with Lord. It can be an indication of a lack of trust and vulnerability in the overall parent-child relationship. The sixteen-year-old who is hesitant to discuss his or her spiritual health was probably equally hesitant to talk about other important subjects with Mom or Dad in earlier years.

As Sheree discussed in the last chapter, a strong bond of affection, trust, availability and initiative in the early years builds a bridge of communication. This bridge will carry the weight of whatever significant discussions are needed concerning their relationship with the Lord.

Our daughter Jaime made her commitment to Christ when she was seven years old. When she was ten, we wanted to be sure that she understood this decision and that her walk with the Lord was deepening in preparation for the upcoming adolescent years. We knew that she was at a stage in her life (usually nine to twelve years of age) when Christianity could simply become learned childhood behavior and habit rather than an ongoing, growing relationship with Jesus Christ.

Sheree and I took the opportunity one evening some months back to ask her some questions.

"Jaime, do you remember the night you asked Jesus to come into your heart and forgive your sins?" I asked.

"Oh, yes."

"That was an important decision you made, wasn't it?" She nodded in agreement as I continued. "Mommy has been talking with you lately about the way you will soon be changing from a little girl to a young woman, right? Well, this maturing process isn't just physical; it's also spiritual. Just as there are changes beginning to happen physically, there is a need for some spiritual changes to come."

"What do you mean?"

We went on to explain to Jaime that we had always been blessed by her love for the Lord and her enjoyment of involvement in the church. We commended her for her willing obedience to give a portion of her allowance into the offering, for enthusiastic participation in worship and for regular requests for family worship times or Bible reading. We then began to explain that her emergence from childhood into adolescence would mean that her relationship with the Lord could begin to take on new meaning. Her worship could become more expressive and thoughtful. She could begin to develop a consistent devotional life. She could look for ways to serve others in the church through things like babysitting for short amounts of time or helping in the nursery on Sunday mornings. Rather than always being taught, led and served by adults, she could start to consider ways in which she could pursue her relationship with God and others by her own initiative.

This turned out to be a meaningful conversation with Jaime. We prayed for her to experience a fresh anointing of God's power in her life. It was a memorable and moving evening, with Joshua sharing how a similar experience years before had deepened his relationship with the Lord. Since that time, we have seen some exciting changes. Her participation in worship has taken on new meaning as she is learning to respond from her heart to the words of the songs, rather than simply enjoying the music. She has suggested some ways in which she can serve others more regularly. We're seeing our little girl begin to make the switch from her childhood responsiveness to God to a mature, heartfelt devotion to Him. What a thrill!

Our discussion with Jaime was natural and comfortable because of the many times we have talked about whatever was happening currently in her life—her need to be more thorough and hard-working in her household responsibilities, her frustrations with some relational difficulties with neighborhood children and the fun she had at a friend's overnight party. The bridge of trust and communication— built brick by brick from her earliest years—is strong enough to support the more weighty matters that her age and maturity are now requiring.

Even from the early years, we parents can nurture in our children a hunger for the Lord. What, then, are some practical steps to accomplishing this goal?

Nurturing Their Hunger for God

First, we can develop the faith pictures we spoke of earlier—visualizing our children as strong, devoted Christians and then leading them gently in that direction. We first came across this principle in the book *Blueprint for Raising a Child* by Mike Phillips. He describes the steps we can take to train our children from faith pictures to reality:

> [Faith pictures] mean far more than daydreaming about what would be "nice." A builder's visualizing must lead

to actual sketches which eventually find their way onto
the drawing table. . . . So parents must visualize actively
and concretely in order to [determine] what they see
God building in the life of their child. . . . This is no time
for wishful thinking. Being "decent parents" and "loving" our children is not a sufficient goal to yield a work-
able plan.

This process can be illustrated by Joshua's desire to be
involved in evangelism when he was five. Sheree and I began
to visualize him in situations where he would share his faith
with others. We knew that this would require qualities like
confidence, boldness, sensitivity and compassion. We began
to encourage him to initiate conversations with waitresses
or grocery store clerks in our presence. We allowed him to
take the money and check to pay for dinner at a restaurant.
We asked him to approach a department store clerk to ask
where he could find various items. Our faith picture of him
sharing the Gospel motivated us to begin in little ways to
cultivate the necessary character qualities he would need to
fulfill this call, should God issue it.

Second, we can nurture our young children's hunger for
God by creating an atmosphere of spiritual warmth and re-
ceptivity in the home. For starters, it might mean having
family worship times, reading Bible stories and listening to
Christian music. Creating an atmosphere conducive to spiritual growth requires creativity, going beyond these things
we would naturally think of.

This kind of environment can be enhanced by maintaining
an orderly, peaceful home where stress is minimized and
family conflicts are less frequent. We can also capitalize on
our children's teachable moments—those sometimes inconvenient times when they show an interest in something

about Jesus or their relationship with Him. Using daily happenings as opportunities to express thankfulness to God—
while shaping Play-Do, folding laundry or spending some
quiet time snuggling—encourages them to include God in
their everyday lives.

Third, we can nurture our children's hunger for God by
providing regular spiritual instruction. This means more
than making sure they are familiar with Old Testament he-
roes. Our aim must be to train them in godly living, promoting the Bible as their guide for life. Family devotions,
children's music tapes, devotional books as they begin to
read and topical studies—the fruit of the Spirit or creation
week, for example—are excellent ways to provide this instruction.

The parents Sheree and I know who are the most effective
in spiritual training are those who have assumed the responsibility as their God-given privilege and haven't delegated it
to others. Churches and Christian schools can be helpful
supplements, but *we* have the mandate from God to "train
our children in the nurture and admonition of the Lord."
Remember, Paul's confidence in his disciple Timothy was
not due to the influence of his youth pastor or children's
ministry teacher, but because of the excellent instruction
Timothy's own mother and grandmother provided for him
(2 Timothy 1:5).

Even church involvement should be designed to support
the parents' role in our children's relationship with the Lord.
Some ways our congregation has attempted to do this include: devising age-related curricula that coincide with our
church's teachings and provide parents with ideas for follow-
up at home; including the children in the Sunday worship
time, followed by children's ministry during the message
time; providing parents with a cassette tape and written

guidelines to lead their children to salvation; and encouraging a lot of parental involvement in the youth ministry.

Before going to the fourth point I'd like to speak to fathers for a moment.

Although the responsibility for raising spiritually mature children is shared by both parents, we fathers must embrace our God-given mandate to manage our households well (1 Timothy 3:4). As husbands and fathers, we are called to provide leadership and oversight of our family's spiritual health. With this calling come the grace and wisdom from God to fulfill it.

For too long, women have been left to try to keep churches and families strong. For their efforts, we should be grateful. The time has come, though, for us to resist any renegade tendencies to leave the spiritual growth of our children to their mothers. Our children need us. A pastor-friend of mine recently put it this way:

> Over-delegating to Mom or the church what God has laid at our feet pits us awkwardly against the Lord's plan for us. Our heavenly Father challenges us to renew our thinking, realign our priorities, and—if the shoe fits—repent of selfishly dodging our responsibility. He's given us a job to do: "Fathers, do not exasperate your children; instead, bring them up in the training and instruction of the Lord" (Ephesians 6:4). Though our wives obviously play a vital role, we're the ones who will give an account [to God].

Dads, time is too short for us to run from this responsibility. Our children's future is too important to risk their spiritual maturity by spending our time pursuing pleasure and material gain. Let's not leave our children's need for instruction, prayer, discipline and church involvement to our wives. Their future relationship with Jesus depends to a large extent on our willingness to disciple them into having a heart for Him.

Fourth, our children's hunger for God can be enhanced by persevering through seasons of spiritual apathy or disinterest. We have already mentioned that children will tend to experience seasons of ebb and flow in their pursuit of God. The question to ask ourselves is not "Is my child as spiritually mature as I would like?" but "Is my child more spiritually mature than at this point last year?" As healthy children grow, their physical appetite increases (boy, are we finding this out!). Similarly, as they grow spiritually their appetite for God should increase. If not, we must look for evidence of sickness in their relationship with Him (harmful influences, for example).

Our perseverance during apathetic seasons should have, as its goal, to teach our children to live by faith and not by their feelings. Like us, they will not always *feel* God's presence. They may not *feel* like participating in worship. We can be tempted at such times to entertain anxious thoughts about their relationship with the Lord, to lecture them or to give in to their desire to curtail their involvement in the church. Such reactions are usually motivated by fear and only accentuate their tendency to live by how they are feeling.

Rather, we must do our part to minimize their feelings and encourage their faith. To a tired child who doesn't like getting up early on Sundays, you may want to say: "Honey, I'm sorry you don't feel like getting up and dressed. I feel that way sometimes,too. But, as with the many other things we do as a family, being with the Church on Sunday is a privileged part of our life together. So get up. Your breakfast is ready, and you need to be dressed in thirty minutes." You can then look for ways to cultivate your child's appetite for getting to know God and His people.

How do we know the difference between a season of disinterest and the beginning of a serious decline? Look for any symptoms of disease in their spiritual appetite: peer dependence (especially on friends who do not share your values and standards); worldly desires, habits or activities; harmful influences (media, friends, entertainment); withdrawal from family activities and relationships. Such things can steal our children's hunger for God by filling them with counterfeit feelings of worth or fulfillment, and require our prompt attention.

The absence of these things indicates seasonal interest that can be overcome by discerning parents.

Praying with Your Children to Receive Christ

At some point, every Christian parent desires to experience the fruit of their example and see their children make a commitment to Jesus Christ. We suggest the following steps to this end.

1. Discern your child's readiness.

From an early age, many children will begin to ask questions about the Lord. At some point, they will begin to show an interest in becoming a Christian. Evaluate whether their interest has been sparked by something like a friend or sibling's salvation, a desire to participate in some ceremonial involvement in the church or genuine desire.

2. Respond positively to any interest.

Even if you question your child's readiness, affirm his or her interest. Here are some questions children ask frequently and some suggested responses.

- "Daddy, am I a Christian?"

  "No, not yet. But someday you will become a Christian. Asking that shows me that you love Jesus very much and that we need to talk more about what it means to give your life to Jesus."

- "Mommy, when can I become a Christian like [a friend or older sibling]?"

  "I'm so glad you want to become a Christian, honey. That's the most important decision you'll ever make. And we'll be happy to pray with you when you can understand why you need to be forgiven of your sins and what it means to become a Christian. We'll talk more about this real soon, O.K.?"

- "Why do people become Christians—do they have to?"

  "The answer to that question is yes and no. No, they don't have to become Christians if they don't want to. God doesn't make people obey and love Him. But yes, we all have to become Christians to have a friendship with Jesus and be forgiven from our sins. Are you feeling a desire to become a Christian?"

3. Discern your child's ability to understand his or her need for forgiveness and to make a sincere commitment.

Many parents are quick to respond to their children's sweet desire to become a Christian. Yet we must resist the temptation to allow our young children to pray a premature prayer. In later years, it will be critical that their commitment to the Lord be sincere and genuine. Ask your child questions like:

- Why did Jesus have to die on the cross?
- What do you think sin is?
- Have you ever sinned? How?
- How does Jesus' dying on the cross pay for your sins?

- What do you think the word *forgiveness* means?
- Does becoming a Christian mean you will never sin again? What should happen when you do?

Age-related questions like these (worded in a more mature way for older children) help us discern the timing of our children's readiness. Our goal is not that they understand the Gospel as an adult would, but that they are aware of their need for forgiveness and why Jesus is able to provide it.

4. Seize the opportunity to pray with them.

The day will finally come when your child is ready to be born again. Whether by your or his initiation, try to be prepared. Rehearse in your mind the confirming questions you will want to ask (similar to those above). And then lead him or her in prayer of repentance and commitment something like this: "Jesus, I know I am a sinner. Please forgive me for my sin and come into my heart. Help me to obey my parents and You, and to share Your love with others. I want to follow You for the rest of my life. Thank You for forgiving me and making me a Christian. Amen."

5. Celebrate the experience.

Celebrating helps to seal the memory. You may want to have a special dinner or outing. Encourage your child to telephone another Christian relative or friend to share the news. Interview him or her about what happened on cassette or video, or document the experience in a diary or on paper to file away safely for his or her future enjoyment.

6. Follow up with lots of encouragement and discipleship.

After the conversion, look for fruit to affirm and encourage ("I've noticed how unselfish you've been lately. I'm sure it's because Jesus lives in you now!"). Depending on his or her age, consider how you can begin to disciple your child in character. Consider beginning to spend some special time alone with him or her on a regular basis for encouragement, instruction and discussion of any questions about Christianity.

When our fourth child, Joseph, was four years old he began to ask questions like those above, which indicated a growing interest in becoming a Christian. We answered his questions and affirmed his desire to know Jesus, but felt he wasn't ready to make a sincere commitment. A year later, when Jesse "made Jesus boss of his life," Joey's interest resurfaced. Again, we assumed his desire was based on his brother's conversion and the joyful celebration that followed. His responses to some questions confirmed our thoughts.

Several months later the topic in the children's ministry on Sunday morning was the death of Jesus. They discussed why Jesus died and how His death makes forgiveness available to us. In following up on this, I saw that Joey was beginning to understand the Gospel—the reasons behind the death and resurrection of Jesus.

Over the following months, Sheree and I talked more with him about what he was learning. We answered his questions. His older siblings, realizing what was happening, read stories to him about Jesus and offered their insights to his questions.

"Mommy, I'm ready to become a Christian," he stated emphatically to Sheree one morning.

"You are? Well, that's wonderful, honey. I'll tell you what. When Daddy gets home, why don't you ask us if we can talk about it after dinner. O.K.?"

"O.K., Mommy," he responded as he ran outside to play.

When I drove up, Joey met me on the sidewalk. "Daddy, can we talk about becoming a Christian after dinner tonight?"

After dinner he offered a reminder: "Don't forget about talking about becoming a Christian," he said.

Joey was waiting in the living room when the dinner dishes were done. I asked him some questions he had been asked several times in recent years and there was a difference in his answers. I didn't want to put words into his mouth or overly prompt him about the answers, so I was careful to phrase my questions in ways that his five-year-old mind could understand.

"Well," I responded, "you've certainly been learning a lot about the Gospel, Joey. I think you're ready to become a Christian!"

"Oh, goody! You mean now?"

"Yes, son. Now."

By this time Jaime and Jesse had joined us in the living room. Joshua had gotten the videocamera and was standing discreetly outside of Joey's vision. We were all aware of what a special moment this was. The prayer of our five-year-old that followed our prayer of thanks to God for bringing us to this moment left us all in tears of joy:

> Jesus, please help me to obey You and forgive me of my sins. Help me not to disobey and please come into my heart. Can You forgive me? And thank You for making me a Christian. Amen.

Every minute spent disciplining, encouraging, instructing, praying for, playing with or worshiping with our son seemed minimal in comparison to the blissful experience our family shared that evening. No event in this life compares with the fulfillment that comes from seeing our children receive new life in Jesus Christ, whether they are five or nine or seventeen. No venture, promotion, career or purchase can bring the joy that comes from watching our children begin the lifelong journey of serving God.

Conversion is actually both the start and the finish. It is the ultimate goal of all that we do as parents. Yet it is only the start of a race that will take a lifetime to complete. Someday, as we see our participation in the race coming to an end, we will pass the baton our generation is carrying to the generation we are raising. What a thrill it will be to see the hands of our children reaching out, their bodies poised to sprint and their faces glowing with confidence!

Jesus, help us to give ourselves to this end.